OE'R THE LAND OF THE FREE

Samuel Lombardo

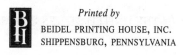

Printed by
BEIDEL PRINTING HOUSE, INC.
SHIPPENSBURG, PENNSYLVANIA

Printed by
Beidel Printing House, Inc.
63 West Burd Street
Shippensburg, Pa., 17257

ISBN: 0-9677051-0-X

Library of Congress Catalog Card Number: 99-97673

PRINTED IN THE UNITED STATES OF AMERICA

Dedicated to my father, mother, and wife.

*My mother for bringing me into this world,
my father for bringing me to America,
and my wife for all her support in writing this book.*

**HEADQUARTERS THIRD BATTALION
394TH INFANTRY
OCHSENFURT, GERMANY**

MAY 11, 1945

Dedicated to the members of Company I, who made the first American Flag in the 99th Div. to fly in Germany.

FULL MAST

I am an American Flag.

From where I fly, I can look down on the boys who made me. Fingers, that a few weeks ago were squeezing triggers and pulling pins from hand grenades, put me together.

For awhile I was just separate pieces of colored cloth scattered on the floor of a bombed out factory.

Now, I am beautiful. My stars are not exactly uniform and my stripes may be a little out of line, but to my boys, I am "Old Glory".

I fly from full mast on the highest tower in the city of Ochsenfurt, Germany. Each morning promptly at 0630, I am hoisted with impressive ceremony, a symbol of democracy and freedom to these boys of mine who fought and died for all I represent.

As they pass by, their hands come up in a snappy salute.

All day I fly over this city, a conquered city, conquered by men of the same calibre as those who made me. The day draws to a close, retreat blows and a solid line of khaki snaps to attention; to the colors, and I start to move. Slowly I slide down the flag staff, never taking my eyes from my boys. Reverently I am folded and carried away for the night. Gone for a few hours but never forgotten.

I realize that very soon now I will be replaced by a new flag, but I will still be proud. I was the first American Flag to fly in Ochsenfurt Kriss. I will not be tossed aside like a worn out rag, for I was made by G.I. fingers, the same fingers will pull me back to my pinnacle in the morning. Once again my boys will pass, once again their hands will come up in a smart salute.

Why? I am "Old Glory, The Star Spangled Banner, The Stars and Stripes."

Yes, I am America.

Norman A. Moore (signed)
Lt. Col. Infantry
Commanding

U.S. 48-STAR HISTORICAL FLAG – WWII

AMERICAN PATRIOTISM

"If they won't give us a flag, we'll make one," said First Lieutenant Samuel Lombardo, platoon leader Second Platoon, Company I, 394th Infantry Regiment, 99th Division during the Battle of the Bulge in World War II. The platoon made this United States 48-star flag from scraps of cloth sewn on a white German surrender flag.

When Company I crossed the Remagen Bridge, their flag, only one side completed, became the first American flag in the 99th Division east of the Rhine River. During breaks in the battle, working mostly by candlelight, the flag was completed after two and one-half months, on the banks of the Danube River.

The flag is in the collection of the National Infantry Museum, Fort Benning, Georgia.

CONTENTS

ILLUSTRATIONS AND MAPS

PREFACE

My rifle platoon of some thirty-six men and myself made an American flag under combat conditions, in Germany during World War II. When we crossed the Rhine River at Remagen, one side of the flag completed, it became one of the first American flags east of the Rhine. Both sides of "Old Glory" were completed when we crossed the Danube River.

All my men were outstanding men and represented not only many states and cross sections of American life, but also many religions, including Jewish, Protestant, Catholic, and possibly others. Above all, they were Americans.

My love for America grew with each moment of living here. I believe that having lived the first ten years of my life under the Fascist rule in Italy gave me a deep appreciation of our freedoms and of our symbol, "The Stars and Stripes."

Not seeing "Old Glory" for several months, during and after the Battle of the Bulge, made me so homesick for it, that I tried to get one issued to us through our army channels. When I was told that it was not authorized, I decided that we could make one of our own.

I have included some stories about our experiences along the way while making our flag. My purpose is to reflect on my experiences during my boyhood in Italy, Pennsylvania, and the military in the Battle of the Bulge, crossing the Remagen Bridge, crossing the Danube River, the Trials at Nuremberg and the Occupation. I want to reflect in my own way on a few of the most humorous, hazardous, and unbelievable incidents that do occur under combat conditions. During all of these battles, my men never let up on our ongoing project, that of completing "Old Glory."

If I have missed some names or details about some action, it was not intentional, but due only to the passing of time, and lack of memory.

Our flag is proudly displayed at the Infantry Museum at Fort Benning, Georgia, as a tribute to America and the United States Infantrymen.

PROLOGUE

While growing up in a small Southern Italian village, without the presence of my father, for most of the first ten years of my life, I matured very quickly under the watchful eye of my mother, uncles and grandfather. I was asked to do things not normally demanded of any eight to ten year old boy, and believe that this contributed much to building my character, and strengthening my mind and body.

America was just a far-off place on the other side of the world, when I first heard its name. There was some mystic and indescribable feeling when someone in our village spoke about America. At my young age, I imagined that America was a land with streets paved with gold and its people were happy and free to do as they pleased. It was like a Shangri-La on the other side of a great ocean. Never, in the stretches of my imaginations did I ever think that some day, I too, would be fortunate enough to be an American. The credit for this goes to my father for bringing us here.

As the oppression by the Fascist Regime became more intensified, the feeling to leave the old country and come to America was almost irresistible, and beyond description.

Upon arriving and living in America, it became evident that the freedoms we dreamt about, were not dreams at all, but a reality.

My love for geography and history also intensified, when in grade school, I read about Daniel Boone, Kit Carson, Lewis and Clark, and all the others who helped explore the American West. At times I wished that I too had lived during that period.

I also became more and more interested in the military as I read about all our great generals since Washington. Without them we would not have our nation as we know it today. I became convinced that the military was the place for me. This was where I could contribute the most to preserve our freedom.

I believed and still do, that the Stars and Stripes is the world's best national symbol. It represents not only all of us who live here, but also all the things America stands for. When I decided to make our own flag during combat, I had no idea what the proper size should be. I did know that if it looked in balance, it would be OK. I also know that when the men saw our flag, their morale would be raised, since it would remind them of home and consequently what we were fighting for. I only started the idea and chose its size, but the rest of the credit goes to my men, who not only fought hard under all types of combat conditions, but continued to work on the flag, when time permitted, until it was completed and proudly displayed.

Samuel Lombardo

CHAPTER 1
My Father and Mother

My father, Pietro, born on June 10, 1890, in Caraffa del Bianco, Calabria, Italy, first came to America in 1905 at the age of fifteen. He was accompanied by his two brothers, Vincenzo, age sixteen and Domenico, eighteen. They settled in Altoona, Pennsylvania, where they lived with friends from the same home town in Italy, who had preceded them by several years. Vincenzo and Domenico became homesick after spending one year in the area and returned to Italy, never to see America again. My father stuck it out, although he was the youngest. He continued learning the masonry trade for which he had started his apprenticeship in Italy, and remained in Altoona until 1914 when he returned home to see his mother, who was going blind. During his stay, World War I broke out and he was drafted into the Italian army.

Dad fought in the Alps against Austria and was wounded in the thigh by a dum-dum bullet, the size of a marble. He then went on convalescent leave to his home town, Caraffa. He was there almost six months when he saw my mother, Agata, at the local church. After arrangements were made to meet her in front of her parents, the custom in those days, they became engaged and were married in 1917. During the next two years, my sister Josephine and I were born.

1

During the next several years, Dad was admitted to some ten army hospitals throughout Italy. None of them would remove the bullet from his hip because of its critical location. He was finally discharged from the army and was able to return to America in 1921. In 1926 he again returned to Italy with the purpose of making his permanent home there. He missed America very much and within two months he moved back to Pennsylvania, never to return to Italy again.

The earliest recollections of my dad were sometime during 1926, when he was ready to depart from Caraffa, Calabria, Italy for his final return to America. There was a horse and carriage near our house. All the relatives and friends, some of them crying, were gathered around the carriage to bid him farewell. The carriage would take him to the coastal town of Bianco, some four or five miles away. He would then go by train to Naples where he boarded a ship to America. On departing, he repeated over and over again, "I'll send for you as soon as I can." My mother, Agata, my sister, Josephine, and I, all crying, waved him good-bye. We waited for the next two long years with anticipation to see our new country, America.

CHAPTER 2
My Boyhood in Italy

Caraffa, my birthplace, had a population of about six thousand people, and was typical of all other towns in the region. It was made up mainly of farming people and some craftsmen such as masons, carpenters, etc. Some were land owners and some were sharecroppers. The town goes back to the middle ages and it seemed that some of the large land owners had property passed down from that period too, since they owned most of the better properties. Several of the wealthier people still carried the titles of Barons and Cavaliers. The town gave one the impression, that it was standing still.

We were better off than most people in the town. Mother had several pieces of land handed down from her father. In addition, she bought several pieces with money sent to her by Dad, who was then in America. Each piece of land was purchased for a special purpose. One produced wheat for our bread, one olives for olive oil, one produced fruit, one produced grapes for wine, and one which was up in the mountains produced firewood. The townspeople, although basically poor, were all hard workers. All had a home and had plenty of food to eat. They did enjoy the simple life, by celebrating occasional religious holidays which were always preceded by a parade. The parades were always followed by dancing in the

Caraffa, Calabria, my birthplace, founded in 1341 by the Greeks.

streets, to the music of bagpipes, the only instruments I remember seeing and hearing.

The people's actions were often tempered by the many superstitions of the area, i.e., if a whippoorwill sang at one end of town one night, it was believed that someone at the other end of town would die during the next day. I believe someone died every day. The town's population was about six thousand people, and the birthrate was high. Even with someone dying daily, the size of the town had not changed in years.

With promoting large families, it seemed that it required all to work in the fields to support their families. The only escape from this "catch 22" situation was either to move out to the industrial areas of Northern Italy or to go to America, Argentina, or Australia.

We were one of the few families in town who could afford to wear shoes, and only because Dad was in America and was sending money back to us. According to all the townspeople we "had it made." We wore shoes, we had a large home and all the land we wanted to support us at a high standard of living.

Our town had no electricity and consequently no refrigeration. Nevertheless, our milk was delivered fresh each and every morning. Its arrival was always preceded and announced by the bleating of some ten to fifteen goats coming down the street ahead of their herder. As soon as I heard them, I would take a pitcher, go outside and wait by our door. When the herd arrived in front of our house, all the goats would cluster together, and as by some magical signal, would stop. I would give our pitcher to the herder, who would then squeeze his way through the herd to pick the right goat. He would then pull it by one of its hind legs to the side and began milking. I never did learn how he knew which goat had been milked and which one had not. I guess, after being with them day after day, the herder probably knew each one by name.

After he filled our pitcher, I would give him the lira, and he resumed directing his herd to the next house, and the rest of the houses down the street. I don't know how many houses he supplied, but I know that each day we received our share of fresh milk.

From the time I was eight years old, until we departed for America, each morning began with my taking a small pot of coffee with cream and sugar to my Grandmother Lombardo. She was

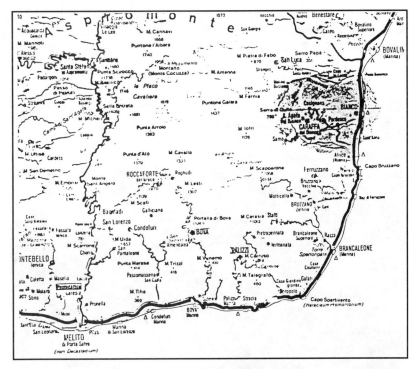

Map showing Bianco, Calabria, seven kilometers from Caraffa on the Ionian Sea (from road map purchased in Italy).

around eighty years of age, partially blind, and lived in a one large-room barrack several blocks from our home near the hearth oven. She was rather tall, large boned, strong willed and insisted on living by herself. Taking coffee to her was the only time I remember visiting her home.

Almost every day, though, she used to visit us, walking slowly in her own way with a cane, and partaking in our meals. She was such a beautiful woman, despite her cataract-covered, half-blinded eyes. Some years after our arrival in America, we learned of her death at age ninety-two.

One spring day when all the flowers were blossoming, the trees budding, and the aroma of the orange blossoms permeated the air, we wanted to get away from class and enjoy the day to the fullest. My cousin Vincenzo, and friend Francesco, decided that after lunch at school, we would make our escape and go after falcons. Vincenzo knew where a nest was located. He had seen the nest several weeks earlier with one fledgling in it.

Ancient farm house on the way to our orchard. (Caraffa)

We took the back alleys of town until we reached the outskirts. Here we found ourselves on a high stone cliff overlooking a beautiful green valley, and the azure-blue sea beyond. The sea was only four or five miles away, but from our perch it seemed unreachable. As we arrived we were so disappointed that we were too late. Our young falcon had already left the nest. The day was still young and we just had to make use of the balance of the afternoon. Vincenzo knew where a mulberry orchard was located. Carefully we began descending down the sharp cliff and before long we found ourselves in the valley below. We continued for another kilometer or so toward the main road that led from the town to all the farms in the valley. A few more minutes found us in the middle of the best mulberry orchard I had ever seen. There were many trees and all were loaded with lots and lots of plump, long, black mulberries.

We decided that the three of us would all climb and eat the berries from one tree. After selecting what we thought was the best and fullest tree, we climbed it. Each one of us chose a different limb and began eating. I don't believe that ten or fifteen minutes had elapsed when I thought that my limb was getting light on mulberries.

My grandfather's former home and my place of birth. (Caraffa)

Beach near Bianco, Calabria, where my mother, two sisters, and I spent our thirty-day vacations each year during my childhood.

Beach near Bianco, Calabria, where I was "attacked" by an eight-inch octopus that came out of the rocks in the foreground.

I asked Vincenzo if I could join him. He said, "Yes," and with a few steps I was again gorging myself with berries from a "better" limb.

I had eaten one or two big mouthfuls, when all at once, we heard a creeping crashing noise, and at the same time felt ourselves falling. The two of us were too much for one limb. It had split and broken away from the tree and we were riding it to the ground. The limb which was about a foot or more in diameter crashed to the ground with a roar. After shaking myself from this scary experience, I looked around for my cousin. I heard a groan and there he was pinned under the limb. I looked up in the tree and Francesco was still up there on his limb, safe and sound.

When I realized what our situation was, I told Francesco to come down off the tree and stay with Vincenzo. I then walked over to the main road to ask for help. I opened an old wooden gate and stood there watching all the farmers and their families returning home from their fields.

At first, only women and small children (under school age) passed by, and I was getting more worried by the minute. I didn't panic, though, since I knew that soon someone who could help would be by. It wasn't long before two strong looking middle-aged men approached with a wagon drawn by an oxen. I ran up to them and told them of my plight. They immediately stopped their oxen, and followed me to the fallen limb.

They both worked so hard to budge the limb a little so that Vincenzo could be pulled out. After some considerable effort and strain, the limb was moved. Francesco and I helped too but I don't believe that our strength was up to the task. Both men carefully lifted Vincenzo and carried him to the awaiting wagon. The oxen moved forward at a slow pace toward town until they reached Vincenzo's home with Francesco and me walking behind.

His father, Uncle Vincenzo, summoned the town pharmacist who after an examination decided that Vincenzo had damaged his ribs, but had not broken them. Vincenzo's chest was bandaged in its entirety with a half white sheet to immobilize it. He then began walking slowly, and all of us were relieved that the injury was not worse.

Francesco and I both left for our homes, happy that neither of us had been injured, and convinced that playing hooky didn't pay.

My sister Josephine spent her free time in the house learning her domestics. When she finished she would go to our balcony over-looking the entire town, and sing. Even at her early age she had a beautiful voice and her goal was to be an opera singer. Every time she sang, she would have an audience within minutes. They would all gather below the balcony to hear her sing the many popular Italian songs of the time.

Josephine and I both attended the local public school which was located only two blocks from our home. The school system consisted of a kindergarten and only a first to fourth grade grammar school. Kindergarten was taught by a teacher from Milan, and teachers from Reggio, the capital of Calabria, some forty miles away, taught us from first through the fourth grade.

The kindergarten building was of Roman architecture, and was the newest building in town. It was situated on a promontory on the northern end of town, not unlike the Parthenon in Greece. In comparison, the grammar school occupied a cluster of World War I vintage barracks, which had been built after the war as low income housing. One grade was taught in each of the four barracks.

There was no electricity, running water or sanitation facilities. The school didn't even have an outhouse. During the recess, or the noon hour, the boys would go outside at one end of the building, and the girls the other. The only privacy provided was the separa-tion provided by the barrack building and a very high bank that ran along the back of all the buildings. With such lack of sanitation facilities, it's a wonder that many of us didn't come down with some serious illness, such as cholera or the like.

Our studies were very intense, with the main emphasis placed on arithmetic. By the end of the third grade, we were required to know our multiplication tables up though ten times ten.

The other subject I recall studying was history. Its emphasis was on heroes of the revolution such as Garibaldi, and the creation of the new Republic in the late 19th century. Spelling was never a problem since most letters in Italian language are pronounced. Usually, if you can pronounce a word you will be able to write it. The math teaching must have been intense, because even today I think my multiplication tables in Italian. "Sette Per Otto – Cinquanta Sei." Seven times eight is fifty-six.

Not many of the older folks could either read or write, for education was not held in high esteem. Usually parents thought that if their children wanted to go on with their education, it meant leaving for the big cities, resulting in another loss of help on their farms.

Mother told us many times how she used to hide the candlelight in her bedroom while trying to learn to read on her own. Her father was very much against women getting an education. In order to prevent any problems in her home, she decided to learn in secrecy, during the night.

Another experience which left a deep impression on my mind occurred during my last year of school there. Recess was over, and all the children were lining up by the door to enter the classroom. My friend and I were at the end of the line and keeping up with the slow-moving line. I noticed one of our boys standing by the side of the door with both hands in his pockets and not making any effort to enter.

As one of our boys who was three or four ahead of us took a step to enter the classroom, the boy who had been standing there stepped up behind him, removed his hands from his pockets, and stabbed the boy in the back with two knives he had concealed. With a flash, he turned around, almost knocking us down, ran down the road as fast as he could, and disappeared.

We learned later that the two boys had an argument during the previous day and this was the way to settle it. Luckily, the knives missed the boy's backbone by some one quarter inch and he survived, but the "Little-Villain" was never seen by any of us again. It was a common practice to send law violators of this type to live with relatives in other towns or provinces. This was accepted as the law of the land, for settling arguments. I have always wondered what the "Little-Villain" of eight years of age ever grew into.

Our weekends were absorbed by going to church, returning home, cooking and eating the rest of the day. The church was several hundred years old, and besides religious services also served as a central gathering place for the townspeople. I did notice that most of the people attending church were either women or children. When I asked one of my uncles why he didn't go to church, he would reply that the smoke from the candles made him sick. I accepted this answer at first, but later on I knew it was not true. Every man I asked gave me the same reply. I came to realize that the responsibility for religious training and good upbringing fell principally on the mothers. There was only one church in the village, the Catholic Church. The mere mention of the word Protestant was regarded as alien and almost against Christian beliefs. We didn't realize what religious freedom was until we arrived in and lived in America.

I spent my free time outdoors, exploring the countryside or visiting one of our pieces of land. Most of the lands were several miles away, so I could use up a lot of energy and time walking.

One of my most vivid outdoors experiences occurred when a man who was working for us, in our wheat field, made a delivery of grain to our cellar, with a mule and a donkey. It was close to noon time. The man told Mother that he was going to the local bar for a bite to eat and would be back soon. He left the animals at our house.

Almost two hours had passed and the man had not returned. A search at the bar revealed that he was in no shape to go anywhere. He had had too much *vino*. Mother began to worry, because the rest of the people working in the wheat field would not know what to do when the delivery man did not return. They were supposed to wait for the man and the animals, and bring back another load of grain when they came home that evening.

Mother called me from playing outside with my neighbors and asked me to get on the mule and take both animals across the river to the wheat field which was six or seven kilometers away. I was to pick up another load of wheat and come back with the rest of the work crew, three men and two women. On first hearing it, the task before me seemed impossible. All the unknowns ran through my mind. Here I am, a boy of eight, trying to take a mule and a donkey to a far away place to which I didn't know the way. The afternoon was wearing on. To say the least, I was scared. My mother gave me encouragement and assured me that I didn't have to worry about a thing. That once we got started, the mule would know the way and would get me to the right place. I felt like Columbus going into the unknown. Mother placed me on the mule's saddle. The donkey was attached to the saddle of the mule with an eight or ten foot rope and followed behind. We were on our way. I held the mule's reins very gently, worried that if I pulled too hard, one way or another, I might misdirect the mule, and end up in unknown lands.

It seemed like an hour before we got through town. Our pace was very slow and never varied. I was beginning to believe by the minute that the mule knew the way. Out of town, we finally reached a trail leading to the river, which was now dry, except for a small shallow stream running through the middle. I was now really much relieved and was more convinced that we were on the right road.

After another half hour or so we reached the dry river bed, and small stream which ran into the nearby sea. The river bed, which was about one mile across, was overgrown here and there with tall evergreen bushes, similar to pines, which are often seen in some of our desert areas of California. We continued at a slow pace through the meandering trail and met no one. The afternoon sun was getting down closer to the mountains and I was getting a little edgy as to how much longer it would be. We were within what appeared several hundred yards' from the other side. To my left, and some fifty yards' distance from our trail, the tall green bushes opened up into a grassy clearing. All was going well, when a wolf, the size of a large German Shepherd dog, appeared at the edge of the clearing.

In a split second the mule reared up and started running towards the far bank, with the donkey loose and running behind it. I don't know how they got untied, but there they were, galloping away, and me on the ground crying. I had heard many stories about wolves but this was my first sighting of one, and I had no idea what he was going to do next. Luckily, he disappeared into the thicket. I didn't stay around that area longer than it took me to get on my feet and start running.

The mule and donkey were out of sight in moments. I knew I had no alternative but to follow their same trail. I cried, yelled and continued running, keeping in mind that a wolf was still loose in the area. It was almost dark by now, to make matters worse.

I breathed a sigh of relief when I heard a voice from the other side. One of the men must have heard me and came to my rescue. He met me and said that both the mule and donkey had arrived at the wheat field and were tied up. He took me by the hand and we walked back to the wheat field, feeling a sense of security. A while passed before the animals were loaded with grain and all of us started back home.

Brush area near River Verde where a wolf jumped out and caused the mule to bolt, making me fall to the ground. (Verde River, Calabria)

By now it was dark. One man led up front carrying an oil lantern. Another followed the rear of the column with another lantern. The animals with their load were in the middle. I walked next to the leader. Once we started back, all five people started singing very loudly and continued singing all the way across the dry river bed. The man told me the reason for the singing was to make enough noise to drown out any noise any wolf would make, so as not to scare our animals. My grandfather had told me about all the wolves in the area and never saw a dead

Breed of wolf that jumped out of the bushes and caused my mule to bolt.

one. The wolves killed lambs almost nightly. Because no one was permitted to have a gun of any type, the wolves roamed at will. The shepherds used large torches made of branches and pine pitch to scare the wolves away when they got too close to their flocks. This was their only defense.

We finally arrived home and unloaded the grain. Mom and I were much relieved and still wondered where the mule driver was. After six hours he was still at large. After the ordeal was over, I felt that his loss was my gain. I had the satisfaction of knowing that I had accomplished a man's job.

As the fall began approaching, so did the grapes ripen. The wine season was soon in full swing. I enjoyed watching my uncles and grandfather make wine. They had their pants rolled up to their knees and barefooted they walked back and forth over the grapes. The grapes filling the big vat which had been carved out of solid rock would soon be crushed. The aroma of the must was overpowering. The juices would flow through a hole carved into an adjacent vat, but at a lower level. Soon the wine was put into small barrels. Two of these barrels were loaded on a donkey and secured by ropes. The wine was then delivered to our wine cellar at home, and dumped into large barrels. This process was repeated from morning until night until the crush was completed.

During the crush in the fall of 1928, when I was nine years old, I was with my grandfather and uncles at our vineyard. In the late afternoon they loaded two small barrels of wine on one of the donkeys. Grandpa told me to start ahead of everyone else and take the wine home. There, someone would meet me, unload the wine into one of the large barrels in our cellar. I remember carrying a pointed stick about a foot long to prod the donkey if he got lazy along the way. It was getting dark and my donkey and I wandered from the vineyard and through our neighboring town toward home.

Our two towns, built entirely of stone and tile, formed almost a solid wall around their perimeters. The only thing that separated the two was a tunnel built through the wall at their border. The tunnel was about one-hundred feet long and on an incline with stone steps leading up to the other side. Then a road, which was the shortcut to our home, followed the solid row of houses all the way. Because it was getting dark, I got a bright idea that I could save time by going home through the tunnel. I started pulling the loaded donkey through and all went well for about twenty-five feet. At that point the tunnel must have been narrower because all at once I found that the donkey couldn't go any further—he was stuck. The barrels were rubbing the walls on both sides and I could not make the donkey move in either direction.

Ancient winery carved out of solid rock. Antonio Bagnara and I are standing in the portion of the winery where the grapes were dumped and crushed by stomping with feet. (Caraffa, Calabria)

Stairs (renovated), formerly a tunnel where I tried to walk through with a donkey loaded with two barrels of wine and got stuck. (Caraffa)

It almost seemed that his legs were dangling in the air. Now, I was really worried. How can I get the donkey out? What punishment will I get when I get home? I may be here the entire night.

It wasn't long until hundreds of the townspeople gathered at the mouth of the tunnel to see the stuck and dangling donkey. What appeared to be a serious problem for me, now became an entertainment for the townspeople. Soon a couple of strong men came to my rescue. They entered the tunnel, untied the ropes from around the barrels, removed the barrels, backed up the donkey, reloaded the barrels, and I was again happily on my way, by way of the main road.

When I arrived home, Mother was crying. She didn't know what had happened to me. When she learned what I had done I got a good scolding and learned my lesson very early in life that sometimes the shortcut may be the longest way there.

The crush was celebrated, usually at the home of my grandfather. This year was no exception. After a very large meal, Grandpa took only me to the rear of the dining room. He then opened a narrow door that led into a large dark room. This was his cheese and wine cellar.

There were five or six barrels, in a row, and all were filled with his different wines. The barrels had been filled only a month earlier, but tasting the wines at this time would give him an idea of their final outcome.

The long room was dark and the only light was provided by the small oil lamp which he carried. He held me by my left hand, while his right hand carried the lamp. We went to the end of the row and stopped at the first barrel. He laid his lamp down, opened the wooden spigot located at the bottom of the barrel's end, and let a small amount of the wine pour into his glass. He took a drink, swished it in his mouth and swallowed most of it. He then gave me the small amount that was left in the glass. I drank it without any problem.

He then proceeded to the next barrel, and the next, and repeated the procedure until we arrived at the end of the row. We had tasted wine from all five or six barrels. We then returned to the dining room where the rest of the family was waiting. By now, I was feeling pretty happy, and not knowing why.

Mother and my sisters were ready to leave. All of us walked out the door and headed for home, which was only several blocks away. It was now getting dark as we were beginning to climb the long stone steps which made up the road. By now my head was spinning and I felt an uneasiness in my stomach. After a few steps, I slouched down on the steps and could not walk any farther. My legs felt rubberized. Mother immediately realized what had happened. Until now she did not know that Grandpa had given me a taste of all his five or six wines. I believe she was more upset with her father for giving me the wine, than my drinking it.

She then sat down on the steps with my sisters and told me to vomit. I replied that I didn't know how. I didn't have to wait long when nature took its course, and I lost the troublemaking wine plus all the food that I had eaten at Grandpa's feast. I felt very relieved that I was not going to die, but I broke out into a cold sweat. Shortly, I felt better, enough to stand up and walk home with Mom and my sisters, happy that this ordeal was over. On the next day when we again visited Grandpa's home, Mother told her dad what had happened the night before, and that he was never again to give me wine in that amount.

Stairs where I got sick from tasting too much of grandfather's wine.

With all the good life, I still left my birthplace with some bad impressions. The most lasting being living under the influence of the Black Shirt Militia, or Fascists. The Fascists were members of the Italian political organization under Benito Mussolini. Their aim was to convert the population to the principles of Fascism, a political philosophy that exalts nation and race above the individual. It stands for centralized and autocratic government headed by a dictatorial leader. It also stands for economic and social regimentation and forcible suppression of the opposition. Their work started out slowly in Caraffa, but eventually had the entire town under their control. This is probably the same pattern followed in all towns and villages until all of Italy was under control of Mussolini, the Fascist dictator. This occurred primarily between 1927 and 1929. We could feel the oppression just knowing that they were around. Our main worry was not knowing what they were going to do next. The oppression gradually grew each year, without the people realizing it.

My first contacts with the Fascists were when they came to our school every Thursday afternoon, and told us that all the boys would get the afternoon off, if we went out and joined in their activities, such as running, jumping and the like. All the boys in the second, third, and fourth grade followed suit and took the afternoons off. It was too good an offer to turn down. Getting the afternoon off was a good deal for us, we thought at the time. The leader of the Black Shirts always had a good turnout.

The leader would take us out along a country road near one of the old stone towers at the edge of town. The towers had been used by the Crusaders to give the signal when enemy ships approached the coastline. He would then line us up in groups of eight or ten and have us run a race of several hundred yards. The worst part of this was that we were to run barefooted. The purpose being to make us strong. Since I was the only one who wore shoes, I had to remove them and run on the old road which was nothing but gravel and large rocks. It was a painful ordeal and not as much fun as I had previously thought.

Even at the age of nine years old, I wondered many times why they were doing this. They were not part of the school system nor the army. It seemed to me that the school teachers as well as the parents were all intimidated by the Fascists. All seemed scared when the Black Shirts were in the vicinity.

After several months of getting the afternoons off, the Black Shirt leader approached us and our parents, and told us how nice it would be for us to buy a black shirt. My mother was a very smart woman and saw through all of this. She did not buy me one of their shirts. For some unknown reason, I didn't want one either. The program was all part of Mussolini's plan to build up support for his Fascist Regime, and get a tighter grip on the population by converting the young.

During this same period two Black Shirts were sent to our town once a month with a film to spread their propaganda. They ran the film near our kindergarten and used one of the building's white walls as a screen. We had no theater or movie house in town.

One evening they showed a film on the work being done by Mussolini with silk worms to improve the silk industry. Another was the drainage of the Pontine Marshes around Rome to make it more productive. At the end of each film it showed Mussolini accompanied by a voice telling us all the good he was doing for the people of Italy. I knew this was all part of the propaganda machine to promote support for him.

At the end of one of these films it showed him signing a decree, with the film speeded up. I was standing next to several old men, and one said to the other very seriously, "Mussolini must be very smart—look how fast he can write."

A number of holidays were now approaching and I remember the Black Shirts holding a big parade. The entire townspeople were out watching, whether by choice or by fear. I always had a feeling, especially during our last year there, that the people had a fear of the consequences if they did not watch their parades. Besides the main body of the marching Black Shirts, other special individuals in uniform would be walking next to the standing crowds who lined the street. These "Specials'" duty was to insure that everyone raised their arm and hand and execute the Fascist salute when the main body of Black Shirts passed by.

I remember very vividly standing next to an elderly man of sixty or seventy years, who was bent over at the waist almost at a ninety degree angle, probably from arthritis or osteoporosis. I do know, he was not able to straighten up, raise his arm and give the required salute when the Black Shirts passed by. One of the Fascists walking along the line of people saw this, came over, grabbed the old man by the back of the collar and yanked him out into the street. I trembled, and felt so sorry for the old man. The last I saw of him, he was being taken away toward the local jail (dungeon) which was only a block away. I never saw the old man again, and have always wondered what fate he may have suffered. I feared the worst, since we heard many stories of the collusion between the police and the Black Shirts and what took place at the dungeon, such as beatings and other forms of punishment. To my amazement no one at the parade route, in the vicinity of the old man, raised his or her voice against the mistreatment, including myself. I could see and feel the fear spreading over the crowd.

The fever of the Fascist movement was running higher and higher as the months passed by during that year. I kept busy with school, and visiting our orchards that were close to town, and tried to stay out of trouble.

At Christmas time of that year Mom received a letter from Dad which said that he had become a United States citizen. We were all overcome with joy. He also told us that we would be going to America sometime during the next year, 1929. I remember receiving a Christmas card showing an old fashioned sled, with a child in it and a boy walking behind and pushing the sled. The ground and road were covered with snow. I didn't see any wheels on the sled and for the life of me I could not comprehend how the sled could move on the road. I thought, "Boy, those American boys must be awful strong." You see, I had never seen ice, and had no idea what it was or what it could do. I didn't know that the sled was sliding on the ice under the snow.

As we moved into the next year, our main concern was when we were going to America. Every month we waited with anticipation. When the monthly letter came from Dad we would gather around Mother and flood her with questions. The letter arrived almost always around the same date each month. Mom was always suspicious of the local postmaster holding out our letters. She would visit the post office, around the first week of each month, and the postmaster would always say, "There is no letter today." Mom would go back in several days and still "No letter today." She then would prepare a large basket of fruit and some cheeses and wine and again visit the post office. On every occasion, as soon as she walked in with the basket, the postmaster would immediately say, "Signora, a letter just came in for you today." Mother had always been suspicious of his coercive behavior, but this was accepted as part of the system. Even if you wanted to do something about it, who would you report him to?

The state had a monopoly over tobacco and salt. One could buy these two products only at state-controlled stores. I could vaguely understand about tobacco, but it was difficult for me to accept the strict controls on salt.

In one case a middle aged man was caught with a large milk can full of salt water from the sea. He was going to dry it out in the sun, resulting in a supply of salt for his household. This practice was against the law. On first offense one would be fined. If the offense was repeated he or she would go to jail.

One of my easiest chores was going to the local state-operated store to purchase our salt. I remember the salt not even being refined, but it came in pieces of all sizes, similar to our rock salt. I would then take it home and crush it with our mortar and pestle, not unlike the ones used in the olden days by pharmacists.

Every time I went to the salt store, I became angry at its practices in selling. I would purchase a kilo, and the extra-large lady behind the counter would place fistfuls of the salt on one side of an old-fashioned scale. On the other side she would place the proper weight. She would keep adding salt until the scale was in balance. I was happy with that, but then she would go one step further. Once the scale was in balance, she would grasp a large fist full from the scale and throw it into a special container under the counter. To make matters worse, she had mammoth hands.

Even as a boy of eight or nine years of age, I sensed that this was not right, but I was scared to say anything about it to this giant of a woman. I would then take the salt home, and tell my mother what had happened. She would tell me that what the lady removed from the scale was her portion, like a tax. I was never happy with the practice. I still think it was a "take" rather than a tax.

During each summer we spent one month on the beach, which was some four or five miles from our home. The area, called The Cape, because of its large rocks and small hill sticking out into the sea, had an adjacent beach extending some two or three miles long. The beach area was still natural and unobstructed by any buildings or other permanent fixtures. Only during the vacation period were thatched huts allowed. These were torn down and removed as soon as the vacation period was over. Grandfather and my uncles would build a hut for us similar to the ones seen on some South Sea Islands, several days before our vacation period started. As soon as Mother was told that the hut was ready, we were on our way.

We looked forward to this time as it was the happiest moment of our childhood. The only unhappy experience during our last vacation there occurred one late afternoon as Mother and all the neighbors were preparing the evening meals. I had played hard all day and swam enough to be satisfied. While waiting for dinner to be ready, I walked out to the water's edge and stood on the only flat rock I could see in the entire beach area. It was probably during low tide. I was looking at the horizon as the sun was just beginning to set over the edge of the sea. I could see the silhouettes of the large ships traversing the Mediterranean.

As I was admiring all the beautiful scenery, I felt something on my leg. I reached down to scratch the area without looking and was horrified at what I felt. I then looked and saw that an octopus had crawled from under the flat rock, and had attached itself onto my leg. I was so startled by it that I could not even yell for help. I began jumping up and down on the rock, waving both of my arms and hands up high. An elderly woman who was outside near her hut adding wood to her fire, saw me in distress and ran right over. She took a stick and with some effort, she removed the octopus from my leg. To my surprise, instead of throwing it back into the sea, she took it over to her hut. She was so happy that she was going to add *calamari* to her dinner. Although it was only a baby octopus I was so relieved to be "saved." I walked back to our hut, to our dinner, without *calamari*. Our vacation was soon over and we were very disappointed that we had to return home.

The political tensions got worse with each passing day. The people were very scared. They were never sure as to what they were free to say or do. One day while walking to the town square I saw a group of ten or twelve men laborers standing in a group near the town fountain. A Black Shirt guard was then with them. They were ready to go to work at one of the neighboring towns. The Black Shirt was counting heads, and then, as they began walking down the road, the guard walked along with them. I asked one of my uncles what was going on. He told me that from now on, all workers working outside of our town would have to be accompanied by one of the

Black Shirts to and from work. I learned later the reason for this was to prevent anyone from leaving the group while en route to work, and participate in some subversive activities against Mussolini. One had the feeling that all the villagers were afraid to talk about the regime, or to do anything that might be considered subversive. Now, I can understand how a nation can be taken over by any dictator, by coercion in small doses at a time. In time it's too late.

On into the spring of 1929, we celebrated the usual *fiestas*. During one afternoon, as I was returning home from one of these *fiestas* I passed a home where there were a lot of people gathered. There was lots of commotion and singing accompanied with a guitar. I couldn't hold back my curiosity. I walked up to the door of the room which housed a large hearth oven. The room was full of people singing and in the corner was an old man playing a guitar. The oven door was open, and inside I could see the body of a man lying on a stretcher. You could still feel the heat from the brick oven, recently fired up and the hot coals removed. The place was like an open house, people coming, looking and leaving. I asked one of the men standing there what the celebration was for. He told me that it wasn't a celebration. That the man in the oven had been bitten by a poisonous spider and that the heat of the oven would draw the poison out. Also, the music and singing would help the man feel better against the heat he was subjected to. I remember the last few words of their song were "and the spider won't bite him any more." After my curiosity was satisfied, I left for home and couldn't wait to tell my mother and sisters what I had just seen and heard. I did wonder whether or not the man was going to make it, and whether the hot oven treatment was a way to go. We did have a pharmacist between the two towns, but no doctor. I wondered what other choices the victim had.

As the summer wore on, the number of Black Shirts around town increased considerably. Everywhere you looked you could always see one or two. Most noticeable was their increase in numbers during celebrations, parades or gatherings of any type. Our biggest fear was that something may happen throughout the country that would prevent us from achieving our dream—that of going to America and joining Dad.

My mother's biggest fear now was of what was happening next. The new drive heard about town was that the Black Shirts were going to search all homes and confiscate all foreign flags found. And who knows what would happen to the occupants. Each day everyone was living in fear about having their houses searched. On learning of this drive, Mother gave me two flags. An American flag which Dad had brought back on his last trip from America and a red flag which Dad had from the days when he supported the Socialist Party.

I didn't know what the red flag meant, but I knew that the beautiful American flag was the flag of our future—America.

Mother folded both flags up into small squares and tied each with a rope to keep them from spreading open. I climbed the ladder up to our fruit bin, holding both flags tightly and very nervously—hoping and praying that no one would come in now. I passed the fruits and vegetables that were spread out and then climbed into the main attic which was at a four or five feet higher level. On the near edge of the attic wall, I passed a large trap, with a caught rat. Its mouth was wide open as if it was squealing for help during his dying moments. His bulging eyes startled me, and I stopped for a moment. I then began crawling on my knee and right hand, clutching both flags under my left arm. I had to be very careful not to slip off the narrow catwalk that led to the other end of the attic. One misstep, or misknee, and I could go through the ceiling. Mother looked scared when she gave me the job. I felt and knew that I was doing this for her. I felt something heroic about it, even for a child of ten.

I finally reached the other end of the attic, which was semi-dark. The only light received was that reflected from the fruit and vegetable area. The roof line didn't permit me to be too comfortable, but I was able to lie on my stomach and hide both flags behind a slanted plank which was anchored to the main house wall and supported the rafters. I then crawled backwards on my stomach until I reached the fruit bin. I picked up the trap with the rat and then went down the ladder to the main floor of the house, where Mom was waiting. We were all much relieved now, since what had to be done was done. Somehow, I felt that I had done a big man's job. There was still that uncertainty as to how far the Black Shirts would go in their searches, when and if they came. What irked me was that I had to hide the American flag. I kept asking myself, Why? Why?

We didn't have to wait long. Within several days the officials appeared on our street, and soon at our door. I remember Mother being very nervous but trying to keep calm. My sisters were at my aunt's. There were three men, all tall, and in civilian clothes. They knocked; Mom opened the door and invited them in. Her voice was weak. They walked in past the stairs leading up to the fruit bin, and stood by the alcove leading to the living-dining room. I don't recall all they said, but there were only a few words exchanged. Then the question came. One of them asked, "Do you have any illegal flags to turn in?" Mom said, "No! But you are welcome to search the house." At the same time I tugged on Mom's skirt and asked her something. I guess I was trying for a distraction and didn't know it. When she tried to keep me quiet, the three men turned around, and left the house. We closed the door with a sigh of relief. Mom and I were still shaking minutes after the door closed. How relieved we were that they walked past the stairs leading up to the fruit bin without even looking up. Now more than ever, we realized that we had to leave for America soon.

As the time for our departure got nearer and nearer, our aunts, uncles, and other relatives visited us more frequently. They spent much time eating, drinking wine and talking with Mother and us three children. My second sister, Paula, was born in 1927, after Dad had left on his final trip to America. During one of those weekend visits, Uncle Domenico, who had made the first trip to America with Dad, was there. I asked him why he didn't stay in America like Dad did. He told me that he missed all the religious holidays that we celebrated almost monthly in Caraffa. Then he said that in America, at Easter time, instead of celebrating the crucifixion of Christ, they celebrated the bunny, and during sometime in November they celebrated the turkey. None of these comments made sense to me at the time, but after being here in America I understood. I realized how things are seen through the eyes of a foreigner who cannot speak nor understand the English language, or the customs of a country.

My uncle's last wish to me was that I eat a banana for him when I came to America. He thought it was the best fruit he had ever tasted, and had never seen one since his return to Italy. I had never seen one either nor even a picture of one, so I had no idea what he was talking about. I did promise that one of the first things I would look for when I arrived in America was a banana.

Finally the long awaited letter came from Dad stating that we would be leaving during the later part of September of that year. We were so happy to receive the good news, but couldn't help have some worries as to what was going to happen to all the relatives we left behind.

The most frequent question asked by our relatives and neighbors was, "Why are you leaving? You have everything here." Our lands, our home, all the food we needed, we even had shoes. Little did they know what Dad had experienced in America—freedom, and a better way of life.

Several weeks before we were to depart for America, my cousin, Vincenzo, age seven, and I, now age ten, were playing with a soccer ball next to our cellar. The cellar which occupied the entire first floor of our house was divided into two sections. The one contained the wine and was kept closed. The other section was sort of a utility area used for storing wood, tools, and the like. The door would be opened or closed and it didn't matter.

On this day in the late afternoon, the large door was open and Vincenzo and I kept playing ball. Sometimes the ball would roll into the cellar through the opened door. Then we would both run in and try to retrieve it. At one time as we were coming out we were met by our neighbor, Angela, who lived down the street and was on the way to our orchard in the country. She was about sixteen years of age and beautiful beyond description. Her brown eyes twinkled and her form was more than her age would indicate. She asked what we were doing. I told her that we were playing ball, and if she wanted to join us. She declined, but asked if we didn't want to play house. I said hesitantly, "yes," but asked her what we were going to do. She told us that she would play the wife and we could take turns playing the husband. That she would lie over in the corner, on several sacks of straw, as if waiting for the husband to come home from work. She told me to be first. I was to go out the door and walk in like I was tired, as if coming home at the end of the working day and go to her bedside. I went out the door, walked in weaving here and there, finally reaching her. She said that I looked like I was drunk rather than tired, and to go out and try it again. Vincenzo stood by the door and, I'm sure, wondering what was next in store for us.

I started back in, this time walking more erect and not so overly tired-looking. When I reached her, she had opened her blouse partly down to her cleavage, and told me that she had been waiting all day for me to come home. I asked what I should do next. She told me to lie next to her and rest my head between her breasts. I followed her instructions without much waiting. I couldn't help feel the warmth of her body, and what a comfortable feeling it was. For some reason, I didn't feel right about all this. I felt like we were hiding and playing at some forbidden game.

I don't believe that Angela and I were in this relaxed position for more than a minute, when outside the door we heard a loud call, "Angela, Angela." With that my cousin ran out the door, and almost at the same time, Angela's mother charged into our "secret" room. She grasped Angela by her hand and took her home, scolding her all the way. I stood there somewhat embarrassed, feeling that we must have been doing something wrong. For the next several weeks prior to leaving for America, if I had to visit our orchard, I would take a detour around their house. I didn't want to face

Angela's mother again. I have always wondered that if her mother had not interrupted our game, how much more Angela would have taught me about husband-wife relationships. I also had a feeling that Angela, at sixteen years of age, had played this game before.

Within several weeks, a horse and carriage came to take us to Bianco, the coastal town, to meet the train. We wound down the gravel road past the medieval tower where the Black Shirts first took us running. I could not help think how lucky we were to be leaving for America, and freedom.

CHAPTER 3
Trip to America

We arrived at the train station in Bianco, a coastal town, within a half hour, and soon we were on the way to Naples. The train ran along the coastline and we were in sight of the sea for most of the way. I was so impressed with the small fishing villages all along the coastline, and most beautiful of all was Sorrento. Its beautiful bay of crystal blue waters, fleet of small colorful fishing boats, and its stucco, red tile roof houses nestled against the steep cliffs, made some picture. I thought to myself, why do people of such a beautiful area have to be oppressed by government?

After a six or seven hour uneventful train ride we arrived at Naples. We stayed in a hotel near the port, and I'm sure it was not a plush one, since Mom and Dad didn't have that much money to spend on luxuries. This was our first trip of any distance from Caraffa, so while this big city was impressive because of its size and setting, we were very disappointed with the hotel's food. The spaghetti we ordered arrived plain and seasoned only with a to-mato or two on top. I remember that we ate little of it, and filled up mostly on bread. Our fear of the big city was on us, so Mom didn't have any difficulties keeping us close to her apron strings. After two days waiting and processing paper work, we finally boarded our ocean liner, and were on our way to New York. All I could think about was getting to our new country and seeing what it was really like. Our accommodations on the ship were adequate and not plush. We were traveling third class.

The first few days all of us were seasick and didn't wander too far from the cabin. We did stay far away from the dining room. I don't think we, except for Mother, had any food for two or three days. We were finally on our boring twelve-day sea voyage to New York.

The only exciting thing that happened the first week out was when one of those Atlantic storms hit us. For a while, I was the only one left in our cabin. I wanted to see more of the ocean, so I got the idea of opening our porthole. There were five or six large bolts and nuts which secured the round glass port window. However, for some unknown reason the nuts were not on too tight, and I was able to turn them, little by little, and remove them. I placed them on the blanket of the upper bunk as I removed them. Soon I was able to open the porthole door wide open. I then stuck my head out, with my shoulders against the bulk head, and gazed out over the waves, which by now looked like mountains. The ship tossed from side to side, and I being only ten years of age didn't realize what a dangerous position I was in. With any sudden movement I could have slipped out, head first, into the raging sea. I really don't believe that my shoulders were wider than the porthole. With each minute the waves were hitting higher and higher on our ship, and several times I could taste the salt spray on my lips. I believe our porthole must have been on the first row of cabins above the water line. Soon a ship's steward opened the cabin door and was shocked when he saw the porthole opened, and me dangling out. I didn't hear him come in. The first thing I felt was being pulled back by my legs and feet. He immediately closed the porthole cover and tightened all the nuts with the large wrench he was carrying. By this time my mother and sisters arrived from their walk, and the steward told Mom what a dangerous thing I had done, and to insure the porthole remained locked. After giving me a scolding, Mom began crying, probably from the relief that I was safe, and our cabin had not been flooded.

The rest of our ocean trip was without incident, until the last day before our arrival in New York. It was still in the twilight of dawn when I awoke. I noticed the rest of the family was still asleep. I hurriedly dressed, and quietly left the cabin, making sure I didn't wake anyone up. As I walked up the stairwell and on deck toward the bow of the ship, I could hear how excited everyone was, and talking about the ship's arrival and seeing the Statue of Liberty. I worked my way up to the bow, hoping that I would be among the first to see the "Lady." All around the large, round, mushroomlike post that was located not far from the bow were ten or twelve young men milling around. All teenagers, probably nearing their twenties, they wondered what a small boy like me was doing there so early in the morning. I told them that I wanted to see the Statue of Liberty. With all of them lining up along the rail I would not be able to see much, even when the sun came up. I asked one of the young men to lift me up to the top of the post. Several of them grabbed me and happily placed me on top. It almost gave me the feeling that I was their mascot.

What exhilaration I had, once I sat on my perch. I thought now that I would be one of the first to see the Statue. Soon the twilight blossomed into dawn and we could see the New York skyline coming into view. The excitement was unbearable as all of the young men looked in different directions thinking that each would be the first to see the Lady. No one really knew where to look except in the general direction of the city's skyline. Slowly, as we moved through the channel we got closer and closer and right before our eyes, bigger than life, was our Statue of Liberty. I inhaled every second of the moment and all the young men in the area began yelling, "There she is! There she is!" I felt like Christopher Columbus looking for the new world and finding it. Being one of the first persons on the ship to see the Statue of Liberty was a real thrill.

These few moments of exhilaration were soon dampened by a reality of the moment too. We could hear a lot of commotion behind us, and people were saying that a small boy had been lost. As I slid around on my seat, I looked down into the crowd and could see my mother walking towards the bow of the ship in tears. As she arrived near the post where I was sitting she looked up, and I know she was quite angry and relieved at the same time. The bigger boys took me off my seat. Mom grabbed me by the hand and led me back to our cabin, while at the same time giving me a good talking to. I'm sure I gave Mom a scare, but I was so glad that she did not arrive any time earlier, or I would have been denied my greatest moment of our sea voyage. We arrived at our cabin and remained there the rest of the day.

Once we docked we started to get processed for debarkation which was to take place the next day. The next morning everyone got up early, had our "gourmet breakfast" and then began our feared processing. I don't know why, but everyone felt uneasy about being interviewed by the dark-uniformed inspectors. How terrible it would be to be sent back to your homeland after coming this far, if you didn't pass inspection.

We went through the medical processing first. This included their looking at our records and checking our chests and breathing for possible signs of tuberculosis (TB). TB was the disease that everyone feared most. All our family passed with flying colors, and we were permitted to go to the next station.

The second phase of our processing was also very scary. This phase pertained to our literacy. I remember my sisters and I hanging on to Mother as we approached the examiner. I pulled on Mom's skirt and reminded her that Altoona had two o's in it. When the examiner asked where we were going to, mother answered quickly but very nervously, "Altoooona, Pennsylvania," insuring that she pronounced the long o's. I don't know whether this examination was for literacy or to insure that we were heading in the right direction. We finally passed, and were so relieved that we could stay in our new

View from lookout at top of Wopsononock Mt. In the distance can be seen our home in Juniata Gap, and Altoona, Pa.

Courtesy of Parks Poultry Farm

country, but the sight of the awesome dark-uniformed and tall guards lingered in my mind for a long time. This was Ellis Island.

We finally met Dad as he came on board to pick us up. We were so thrilled even though our recollection of him had to be reinforced by looking periodically at his photographs that Mom was carrying. It had been more than two years since we last saw him. This was also his first sight of my sister Paula, since she was born after he left Caraffa, on his last trip. As we completed going through the lines leaving the ship, we headed toward the railway station. I was awed at seeing stores and the like all underground. I couldn't believe I was seeing so much activity and so many people. This was New York City. As we reached the station platform, I experienced my first scare in our new country. I saw my first black person. He wore a red cap, had a dark blue uniform and came right at us, with what appeared big, bulging black and white eyes. He wanted to carry our bags. It was really a shocker to me since I had no knowledge of any black people existing anywhere. My father assured me that they were okay, and would not hurt us. They immediately picked up our baggage; we boarded the train and we were on our way. We arrived in Altoona on 3 October 1929, and all of us, except Dad, were surprised at how cold the weather was for October. I'm sure it wasn't lower than probably forty degrees, but that's the coldest we had ever experienced in our lives. The friends with whom Dad had lived, when he first came to America, were at the station to greet us and to take us to our home in Juniata Gap, a suburb several miles north of the city.

My mother, sisters, Paula and Josephine, and I, soon after our arrival in America. (Juniata Gap, Altoona, Pa.)

We rode in their new Nash automobile, and already feeling like a million.

As soon as we arrived, the first sight that confronted us was our flooded cellar. It was full of water almost clear up to the first floor of the house. Dad had made plans to build a large stone house with a one-and-half-story stone garage and guest house. However, as the year was nearing an end just prior to our arrival, the economy came to a standstill, and culminated with the crash of the stock market in mid-October 1929. This was the beginning of the Great Depression. I guess, we could not have arrived at a worse time, but we felt so lucky to have made it before conditions in Italy got worse, and could possibly have prevented our departure.

CHAPTER 4
Growing Up in Pennsylvania

ecause things had not gone as planned for Dad, he stopped
all construction of our new house. He put all his efforts in
improving what he had already built, the garage. He started
all the improvements about thirty days before our arrival. In this
short time, he added a kitchen and dining room on the back. He
made four bedrooms out of the upstairs area, and replaced the two
large garage doors with a wall, large windows, and a standard size
door. The major part of the garage area became the living room,
and the remainder a bathroom with shower. Dad told us that he
had finished plastering the last room the night before he left for
New York to meet us. He did not have time to dig a drain for the
cellar. A big rainstorm came while he was in New York, and filled
the cellar to its full capacity.

A large pot belly stove stood in the middle of what was now
our living room area and was the sole provider of our heat for that
part of the house. Our bedrooms were warmed by heat which traveled upstairs from the cellar through a pipe in the stairwell. Dad
also had cut a hole in the kitchen ceiling above the stove. This helped
carry a little heat to my bedroom which was located directly over
the kitchen. The dining room, located right next to the kitchen, received its only heat from the kitchen stove. These accommodations

were far from what we had left in the old country, but we could not be happier than being together with Dad and to be in America.

Dad's first priority was to dig a ditch and drain the cellar. I helped with the digging and within several days we had a dry cellar. We rested for several weeks, and got acquainted with our neighbors and our surroundings. Soon, all of Dad's friends, including the ones from the Italian community, came out to the country to visit us. One of them brought me a silk handkerchief in the design of the Italian flag. She told me to fold it into a triangle form and wear in my shirt pocket.

Thirty days elapsed before we knew it. We didn't know any children going to school, nor did we know one word of English. A day before the thirty days were up, a constable come to our door and reminded Dad that Josephine and I were to start school the next day. We were very scared of the unknown, since we had no idea what to expect.

The next morning Dad walked down to the school house with us, and introduced us to our teacher, Miss Adams. He remained a little while and then left. We met all of the kids and played with them during recess. While playing, one of the boys came up to me and pointed to my shirt pocket and I guessed he wanted to see what I had. A chill went up and down my spine and I was scared stiff. I feared showing him the Italian flag handkerchief. I just knew I was going to go to jail for having a foreign flag in my possession. I was somewhat relieved when Miss Adams took my hanky and showed it to all the class. I guess she wanted them to know what the Italian flag looked like. I couldn't believe that no one did anything to hurt me. Could this be what Dad was talking about when he told us about freedom in America? What a relief and great feeling. When I got home that afternoon, I told Mother what had happened, and she was happy too. Even though it was safe I put the handkerchief away and never brought it out again.

We didn't realize what religious freedom was, until now. Dad had just built a beautiful stone church just a half mile from home

Church that my father built in America, just prior to our arrival. Money he received from this work enabled him to pay for our trip to America. (Juniata Gap, Altoona, Pa., circa 1928)

and across from our schoolhouse. It was the Methodist Episcopal Church. Father reminded all of us that there was only one God, and that it didn't matter how we prayed, as long as we prayed. Mother wasn't convinced, but both of us children and Dad attended his church for more than thirteen years, until we moved to California. Mother prayed at home and attended the Catholic Church, when on rare occasions we went to the city. It was difficult to imagine that we had more than one church, more than one religion, and we could attend whichever one we chose. This was religious freedom. This was America.

The weather was getting colder and colder by the day. By early November we had our first snow. Mother felt so isolated out there in the country. Dad had bought this wild piece of land away from the Italian community because he wanted us to Americanize as quickly as possible. While the location was great for Dad and us kids, it must have been very difficult for Mother. She didn't know anyone, and had no one to talk to.

This situation soon changed. The PTA sent a lady out to our home every Thursday evening to tutor Mom. She would spend an hour or so with her, then we would join in and practice together. The lady covered only simple words and basic sentences, but I know it was a great help for all of us, especially for Mother.

I felt so fortunate in attending our first school in Juniata Gap. The building was a one-story wooden structure, with a bell steeple, the style you see on old post cards. The bell tower was directly over the front door, giving the school a New England church appearance. The interior was one large room with four double rows of seats, one double row for each grade. I was placed in the third grade and my sister Josephine in the fourth grade. A large pot belly stove occupied the front central part of the room. The blackboards covered the entire front wall. The outhouses were unheated, four-holers, one shed for the girls and one for the boys, widely separated and built next to the back fence of the school property and near the playground.

Miss Adams was a middle-aged lady with long reddish hair, not unlike one of the portraits by the Dutch painters. What a gem of a teacher she was. She would give the morning assignment to each class, then move back to the first row, first grade, and spend a half hour or so teaching that grade. She would repeat this all day, so that everyone was kept busy, either studying or being taught. The discipline was remarkable. Everyone remained calm and quiet even when Miss Adams was teaching one of the other three grades.

My greatest appreciation of her teaching was when she took time out daily to teach my sister and me such simple phrases as "Open the door," "Ring the bell," and so on. After several days of practice she would call on us to execute the actions required. This was our introduction to the English language. Soon these few phrases expanded to longer ones and each day we looked forward to her calling us for additional tasks.

The creek which ran along the back of the schoolhouse had its origin several miles to the north at the base of a mountain. This same creek formed the back boundary of our property. Our house was located about a mile from the schoolhouse and all of us walked to school. During our first winter, I walked to school on the frozen creek, while my sister took the road in front of the house. I learned what ice was at last. How exciting and exhilarating those walks were.

Neighbors Vernon Gibson and John Folk help shovel snow in Juniata Gap, Altoona, Pa. (Circa 1937–38)

At times on our way to school the stillness of the snow was broken by the jumping of a cottontail on my left or a deer or ruffed grouse on my right. Taking the creek route to school was exciting but ended one day when I stepped on thin ice and slipped into the water up to over the top of my shoes. By the time I got to school, my pant legs were frozen stiff and my feet chilled to the bone. As soon as I arrived Miss Adams allowed me to take my shoes and socks off and dry out, next to the hot pot belly stove. After that episode I went to school by the road together with my sister "Josie."

Our first winter was a real experience for us. It was very demoralizing knowing that most people were now out of work. Even if there had been work for Dad, he could not work at his trade. All masonry work came to standstill during the winter months. From October through March our main activity was cutting wood and trying to keep the house warm. My principal interests outside the home were hunting, fishing and taking long hikes and exploring the woodlands behind the house. I also carried hay and grains into the woods to feed

Back center, my sister Paula, who was born in Italy, with sisters Agatha, Jeanette, and brother Pete, who were born in Juniata Gap, Pa. (Circa 1939)

the deer and wild birds when the snows got deep, and their food supply was scarce.

Back of the house and across the creek was an abandoned farm. Part of it was a field with an old withered orchard, planted with apple and pear trees. The rest was mostly wooded. The wooded area served as a habitat for many deer, birds and small animals. What a playground for me! How lucky I felt to be able to learn nature and be part of the animals' habitat. I learned to understand direction, nature, and topography. I believe that this experience later played a very important part during my war time activities in Belgium and Germany.

During the next summer a new eighth-grade brick schoolhouse was built about a block down the road from our old school. It was modern and would keep us close to home for another four years, but I really missed the old one-room schoolhouse and Miss Adams, who retired that year. I will always have a warm spot in my heart for her and the old school.

Parks' Chicken Farm (circa) 1929. Farm where I did chores on my way home from school during 7th and 8th grade years. Baby chicks, chickens, and eggs I received in pay contributed much to our family getting through the "Great Depression."

Photo courtesy of Mr. Robert Parks, Juniata Gap, Altoona, Pa.

The new school was called Logan School, after the great Indian, Chief Logan, who years before had resided in the area. Our township also was named after him. We had lots of space around the school, and made full use of it during our recesses and other periods of free time. A high hill behind the school provided our skiing and sledding area during the winter months. My closest friend here was Donald Deffinbaugh, no doubt of German descent. He was a solid, robust boy of my same age and a lover of nature. It seems that he was always in trouble with the teachers. He would, almost on a weekly basis, bring a snake or baby animals to class, hidden in his clothing. Once in a while they got loose in the classroom and scared the girls half to death. The worst time was when he had obtained a litter of young skunks and was trying to raise them at home. The stench was carried to school on Don's clothing, and on more than one occasion he had to be sent home to change his clothes.

After four years at Logan School we attended the D. S. Keith Junior High School for only one year, the ninth grade. The school was located near the center of Altoona, about three miles away. After attending there, we were to go either to the Altoona High School, or the Catholic High School, for the final three years. Going to the Junior High for only one year was not the best. We felt like the outsiders from the country; nevertheless, I felt very privileged. I could now play football, over all objections of my parents. I was chosen president of my homeroom, and with the addition of playing football I really felt I was someone. Most importantly, I was being accepted and becoming more American day by day.

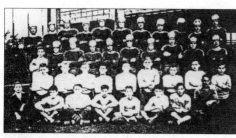

My football team, D. S. Keith Junior High School. (Altoona, Pa., 1935)

During football practice one day, coaches from both high schools approached me and asked me which high school I was going to attend. Each coach wanted me to play for

Author with sisters Josephine and Paula experiencing their third winter in Juniata Gap. (Circa 1933-1934)

his high school. Little did I know that right after our Christmas break I would be quitting school. The depression was now being felt by all, and I felt obligated to work with Dad and help raise my four sisters and brother. My biggest worry was that Mom and Dad were going to have more children. I made my feeling known to Dad and Mother many times by reminding them of those families in Caraffa with twelve and fifteen children who never were able to improve their lives. They both must have agreed with me because we had no more additions to our family.

We worked so hard during the summer. When October arrived, there was always one more person who had an old house and wanted a fireplace built before the winter came. It was usually freezing in October and we had to add antifreeze to our mortar. My fingers would chap and crack from the alkali in the cement. They would then bleed and burn to the limits of my tolerance. It seemed like an eternity until we finished our last job of the year.

The weekends and evenings during the summer were spent in digging our garden area with a shovel. On many evenings, we would have an extension cord with a light, to allow us to dig at least until ten o'clock at night. Because our grounds were all divided into nice rectangular plots with manicured lawn paths running between them, it was not possible to prepare the grounds by hiring a man with a horse and plow. As tough as this work was, it was all worth it. We always had plenty of food on the table. Mother also baked some twenty loaves of bread per week in a large hearth oven that Dad had built for her. Although we were in a deep depression, we always had plenty of food. In addition to the food we grew, and Mother canned, we bought our staples such as flour, olive oil and fruits, including bananas. I did eat a banana for Uncle Vincenzo as I had promised, and liked it.

No sooner had the depression ended, that World War II broke out in Europe. I could see us getting involved sooner or later. On 11 November 1939, I went to the National Guard Armory and volunteered to join. Ironically, "The Old Armistice Day," was being celebrated.

Dad and Mom objected, and were very worried about my joining. I convinced them that if I joined I would be better prepared, and if war came, I had a better chance of survival. I put them at ease as I walked out and down to town on that November 11th morning. The sergeant in charge wasted no time in putting me into a uniform and gave me a few minutes of instruction in the Manual of Arms. Little did I know that he was going to push me into my first parade within an hour or so. It was Armistice Day, and of course a parade was

Fellow workers and I on one of the work projects of the National Youth Administration (NYA). Received twenty-five dollars per month, and helped family get through the Depression. (Altoona, Pa., circa 1937)

held. What an experience! I was so proud to march along with my unit, our flag, and the band.

We marched down 11th Avenue, made a right turn on 15th Street and made another right turn up 12th Avenue in the direction of the armory. Before the parade, I practiced at least an hour or so on how to execute "Right Shoulder Arms." I was happy with myself in carrying the rifle on my right shoulder correctly all the way up 11th Avenue, a distance of four blocks. When we made the turn on 15th Street, our detachment commander, a lieutenant, yelled out, "Left Shoulder Arms." I thought the world would come to an end. How was I to move my rifle to my left shoulder in a military manner? I just couldn't keep it where it was at? I bit the bullet, just reached up, grabbed it by the stock and moved it over to my left shoulder. I'm sure it wasn't a good military move, but I got the job done. We finished the parade without any other problem except I could feel my wrapped leggings loosening up. I was afraid to look for fear that I would see a worse condition than I was feeling, and looking down was unmilitary. We finally arrived at the armory safe and sound, and I was feeling like a real American.

Activities at home continued about the same. Josephine received a scholarship to the Julliard School of Music in New York and soon departed for the big city. My work became more intensive as I got older. It seemed to me that as I worked better at helping Dad, he would hire another mason. At my peak I mixed mortar by hand, carried stones and placed them next to the mason, whether on the ground or up on the scaffold. Supporting three masons for nine or ten hours like this, I was ready for a rest. This pattern continued until February 1941 when my unit, the 28th Infantry Division, was called into Federal Service.

CHAPTER 5
In the Army

I soon found myself at Indiantown Gap, Pennsylvania, a camp not too far from Hershey, Pennsylvania, home of Hershey Chocolate. The air, miles from the plant was filled with the smell of their candy. I was assigned to an intelligence section in a battalion headquarters detachment. As such, I had to master map and aerial photograph reading. I was soon promoted to staff sergeant, with duties of intelligence section chief. I took a liking to military symbols, conventional signs, aerial photographs, and map reading in general. I didn't think it was too difficult. Most of the men in my detachment had been there for years and still could not read a map. As soon as we completed our basic training, I found myself teaching map reading to the rest of the battalion.

Several months went by and we found ourselves on the way to the Carolina maneuvers. During the short several weeks in the field I was able to develop and practice my map and aerial photograph reading with great satisfaction. On one very hot day the battalion commander, Lieutenant Colonel Marlin, gave me the duty of taking the four companies of the battalion and our battalion headquarters detachment, which included himself, to an area several miles from camp. From there, each of our units was to be separated along a road and given their particular assignment, or compass direction, to get back to camp. After about an hour or so march, we reached our designated areas and I gave each company their assigned directions. I kept ours, as I was to lead Colonel Marlin and our small detachment through the woods, and back to camp.

We started out single file down through a draw and woods. Slowly, the woods became thicker and thicker. Before long, we were almost in a junglelike situation. The temperature was hot and almost unbearable. We had

First Day at Indiantown Gap, Pa. (February 1941)

walked almost one and a half hours. Pretty soon we were faced with an uphill climb steeper than I had contemplated, and with junglelike vegetation, which made our climb that much worse. I never knew that in our own Carolinas, we would have a jungle like this. We soon stopped for a moment and I saw Colonel Marlin talking to our First Sergeant Leity. His face was blushed and I had a feeling he was worried. Sergeant Leity came over and told me that the colonel was concerned about the direction we were going. I assured him, that I always trusted the compass and that we were headed in the right direction.

After a few minutes' rest, we continued on our exercise, hacking away at the undergrowth as we struggled up the hill. Within twenty minutes or so, I reached the top and an open field. What a stroke of luck! I knew we were going in the right direction, but not this accurately. We were only about twenty-five yards from Colonel Marlin's tent. I didn't say anything, as the next two or three men reached the top. The colonel was about fourth or fifth in line next to

With my National Guard unit on maneuvers in the St. Lawrence Valley near Ogdenburg, N.Y. (Hqtrs. 2nd Bn. 110th Infantry Div., circa Aug. 1939)

Sergeant Leity. As soon as he arrived at the top and out of the thicket, his eyes beamed with satisfaction. I had never seen a smile like that on his face before. He congratulated me for being so accurate, walked over to his tent and didn't lose any time calling the regimental commanding officer (CO). He told him that he had the best map sergeant in the division and how close I had brought him to his tent. Again, what a stroke of luck. From that day on, I couldn't do anything wrong, when it came to maps and aerial photos. Our two weeks of maneuvers were soon history, and I came away with much more experience and confidence.

On the way back from the Carolinas we stopped and camped in an open field near Lynchburg, Virginia. We were told that there was a Women's College not too far away from where we camped, but to my knowledge no one could get away to visit it. While around the campfire, after the supper chow, one of the men was listening to the radio news and he heard that Pearl Harbor had been attacked. At first no one wanted to believe it, but by the minute, other radios were turned on, and the news was confirmed by other stations. The news spread like wildfire throughout the campground and everyone was wondering what was going to happen next. No one slept much that night. I remember staying up around the fire until 1:30 or 2:00 in the morning listening to someone's radio. After sleeping only a couple of hours we broke camp early and headed back to Indiantown Gap, for refurbishing and further orders.

After several weeks passed, we found ourselves packed and on the move again, this time for Camp Livingston, Louisiana. We now were in for the duration, instead of just one year, as our original orders read. I marked all the maps for the battalion, indicating the

With my father and mother during one of my visits home from Indiantown Gap, Pa. (Juniata Gap, Pa., circa Feb. 1941)

route we were to take, showing all the camping stops along the way. In addition to being the battalion topographical sergeant I was also assigned as assistant driver to Colonel Marlin. The first impressive sight on our trip was going through Washington and seeing all the Federal buildings, including the Washington Monument. The new Jefferson Memorial was just being built or just completed. I stuck my little box camera out of the small canvas opening on the side door and took my first photo of the trip.

One of the highlights of the entire trip was going through the Shenandoah Valley, Virginia. What a beautiful valley! Even though we went through after the completion of the apple harvest, there were still plenty of apples around. The people, young and old, were all out in droves along the road with bushel baskets full of apples. When we slowed down or stopped our convoy, the locals would swarm around the vehicles and inundate us with apples of all varieties. What a treat! The giving really showed the character of the people. What Americans! I knew they were good people, but more importantly, they were supporting us in the war effort. This was our introduction to Southern hospitality.

CHAPTER 6
Camp Livingston, Louisiana

Our arrival at Camp Livingston was somewhat disappointing. The camp was run down and was one of those camps built during World War I, then inactivated, and laid empty all those years. It was now so-called upgraded and ready to receive our division to train for World War II. While there, I studied and continued teaching map reading and map making.

One day I took a group of my men on a map making operation. We hiked for several miles and stopped on top of a small hill. I found out that all hills in Louisiana were low. I had everyone lie behind the hill, overlooking a nearby military airfield. All of us attempted to emulate less than perfect conditions, and draw a panoramic sketch of the runways and buildings. We saw the first B-25 bombers practicing take-offs and landings on a short runway. I later was told that this was where General Doolittle and his pilots practiced their take-offs for their raid over Tokyo later in the war. It was so exciting to watch, but our fun was cut short. Within a few minutes we were surrounded by the provost marshal of the base, a captain and five or six military police. After explaining to him what we were doing and identifying ourselves, he released us without any further complications. He did tell us that this area was restricted, and we were not to return. One thing for sure, I gained great respect for their security.

Several months elapsed as we continued our training when a recruiting drive began for Officer Candidate School (OCS). I applied and within a few days appeared before a board of three officers. One colonel, one major and a captain. I never shined my brass or shoes any harder. My uniform was immaculate. I looked my best, and was very confident. When I appeared before the board my only worry was that I had not finished high school. I kept my fingers crossed and entered the room. I saluted and was told to sit down. The only two questions I was asked were, "Where is the Island of Malta?" and "Where is the Skagerrak?" Being a lover of geography, I answered both correctly and was dismissed. The waiting seemed like forever, but within several days I was notified that I had been accepted and was on the way to Fort Benning, Georgia, and OCS.

CHAPTER 7
Fort Benning, Georgia

My three months at Benning were marked by intensive training and heat. I was there from 14 April to 14 July 1942, during some of the hottest weather of the year. By the time graduation day came, we were in top physical condition, mentally alert and ready to fight. We were taught tactics, familiarity with all infantry weapons, and were very much imbued with the infantry motto "Follow Me," knowing that some day we would be calling it out, in combat.

The scariest moment I believe we had was during the tank training class. We were told to dig our own foxhole. I dug and dug to make sure it was deep enough. When I got through, the instructor called on one of our biggest tanks that was parked over in the woods to move forward. I believe it was a General Sherman tank. It proceeded to run over each one of our foxholes, with us in the holes. I huddled down into the hole and braced for the worst. The tank groaned forward, straddled my foxhole and stopped when it was completely over me. All I could think was, "Why doesn't he continue forward?" He stopped only for a few moments and moved on through. The ground shook and a small amount of dirt toppled in from the sides of the hole, but I was safe. The exercise was to

Graduation Day with classmate Second Lieutenant William McClure, OCS, Fort Benning, Ga. (suntanned author on right). McClure was killed in action while serving with armored division in France. (14 July 1942)

Classmates on Graduation Day, OCS Class 33, Fort Benning, Ga. (14 July 1942)

demonstrate to us how safe we were from a tank, when we were in a foxhole.

Graduation day came and the ceremonies were conducted in one of the post's theaters. Our principal speaker was a Major Woodward who was a Medal of Honor winner, and one of our greatest living heroes from World War I. How inspiring! I was so impressed, I went up to him and asked if he would pin my second lieutenant bar on my shirt collar. He was so happy to be asked and obliged. All of us Shave Tails waited impatiently outside the theater to receive our orders. We milled around for a while, outside the theater, wondering what the future held for us. My orders arrived and read "Transferred to Camp Joseph T. Robinson, Arkansas."

Chapter 8
Camp Robinson, Arkansas

I lucked out again. Camp Robinson was a training camp located just a few miles north of Little Rock, Arkansas. We heard through the grapevine that the people of Little Rock were the best, and full of southern hospitality.

I, along with five other new Shave Tails, arrived at my new station during the next day and soon found out that what we had heard about Little Rock was true. The people were so outgoing and friendly. They planned many activities for the enlisted men as well as for the officers. Included were parties, dances, etc. Every night something was going on in town. The clubs and bars were also flourishing, but the most notable thing was how friendly everyone was. Talk about supporting the troops! Things could not have been better.

I settled in my new duties, and luckily my new assignment was to teach basic training to the new recruits who were now coming into the camp at a steady flow. My primary subjects there were map and aerial photograph reading. The training was performed in cycles of six, eight, eleven, and thirteen weeks. I believe the length of the cycle was determined by the number of replacements and the speed in which they were needed in the overseas theaters of operations. I was happy as a lark with my duties; however, I was anxious to get overseas to help defeat our enemies and end the war. Many levies for replacement officers came and went, and I volunteered for all of them without success. The usual reason given was always that I had a specialty in map reading and could not be replaced. I didn't know why, but almost everyone stayed away from maps, but I'm sure by now that we had many others who were equally or more qualified than I was.

I thought map and aerial photograph reading was easy, and wanted all the men to learn well and maybe feel as I did about the subjects. On many weekends, when all the trainees were free, I would ask for volunteers, and then would take them out on some hilly or wooded area near the camp, and give them a special class on my own time. I would always have ten or fifteen men show up for the field trip. I would show them how hills, valleys and streams were represented on a map by contour lines. The men were very excited as to how easy map reading really was. When they learned how to identify individual trees on an aerial photograph, it was the frosting on the cake. I returned to my company area, always with a sense of satisfaction that I was doing just a little bit extra for my country. Besides my instruction duties I was now assigned as company commander and responsible for some two hundred men.

After the first day of being with my company, I noticed that when we returned to our regimental area after a day in the field, all troops stopped. We remained at attention for a minute or two. When I asked why, my sergeant informed me that retreat was being played by the regimental bugler. "But we can't hear it," I replied. As soon as I reached my orderly room, I submitted a recommendation to the regimental commander. I suggested that a wooden tower be built in the center of the regimental area, tall enough to be above the roof line of the barracks. The bugler could climb up the stairs and play from the platform on top.

Within a week, the regimental commander informed me what a good suggestion I had submitted. The tower was built within several more days. How beautiful the bugle calls sounded the first evening from the new tower. Not only retreat and recall, but especially tattoo and taps, which were played late at night. The calls were not only heard by those nearest the bugler, but, also, the notes echoed all over the camp. After one and one half years of teaching here, we were ordered to leave and open up a new training camp near Tyler, Texas. It was Camp Fannin.

CHAPTER 9
Camp Fannin, Texas

U pon my arrival at Camp Fannin, I was assigned another training company of some two hundred men. As such, I was responsible for training, morale, welfare, etc. All at once I became their father, mother, attorney, clergy, and disciplinarian; or for that matter, anything else the men needed.

In order to learn about my men as fast as possible, I set up a schedule on my own time, after the evening meal, and interviewed five men each evening. I spent only five to ten minutes with each man, but it was worth every minute. I learned a little about the men's backgrounds, and also if anything was bothering them. I then assisted in correcting any problems they were facing.

I tried to instill in them the "Esprit de Corps" necessary to carry them through any battles they would encounter down the road. Besides their daily training, I would give a pep talk on being physically fit and mentally strong, and about our great country. I also included the subject on why we were fighting.

On one occasion, I led the company on a ten mile march with full packs. The men were informed that no one would be permitted to drop out of the march. After completing four or five miles, seven or so men dropped out with a myriad of excuses. They were picked up by the ambulance and taken back to camp. When the remainder of the company and I completed our march, I announced that after supper all the men who dropped out would be going on another march, if they weren't ill.

An hour or so after supper all assembled at the company area, and the first sergeant inspected the men's feet. All men looked well, and were without any blisters. We soon were on our way. I reminded all of them that they could make it if they had no physical defects. After all, I had finished ten miles that afternoon and was going out again. Down deep I didn't like it, but I knew I had to do it. All men completed the march, and I had walked ten additional miles. The men were so happy; they now knew they were as good as anyone else in the company. After putting myself on the line, I knew there was no backing out. I believe all of us benefited from the experience. During the next ten or eleven weeks of training, we had many marches, and I had the satisfaction that no one ever dropped out, unless he became ill—which didn't happen too often.

During one of these training cycles, my company had zero AWOL (Absent Without Leave) rate in my regiment of 3,500 men. I was so disappointed one day when I had the first one. A prisoner from the stockade was assigned to my company from 7:30 a.m. to 5:00 p.m. for training only. One day he ran away from one of the field exercises. He was my first AWOL in six months.

My company on parade, Company "B" 56th Training Battalion, 12th Regiment, Camp Fannin, Tex. (Summer 1943)

It wasn't long until he was apprehended somewhere in Kansas and returned to my custodianship. He was a mere seventeen-year-old recruit from a farm in Kansas.

I had him report to me in the evening, on his first day back, and started a long indoctrination and briefing on the benefits of being an American. Also, the importance of being in the army to defend those freedoms. I covered my boyhood in Italy and told him how restricted we had been living under a dictatorship, how free we were here and how many of us took our freedoms for granted. Some of our people believed that all other countries live like we do. What a false impression!

The boy soon broke down and cried, then told me that no one had ever talked to him like that. That now he had a greater appreciation of the freedoms our country offered us. How lucky we were to live in America. He didn't know that other countries didn't live like us. He then saluted and was escorted back to the stockade. He was brought back daily and finally completed training with honors. I am sure that he was a good soldier no matter where he served after that.

Finally, in October 1944, a request for six officers came to our regiment. The officers were to be assigned to the European Theater of Operations (ETO). The regimental commander approached me and informed me about the levy but that I didn't have to go. That he was going to recommend me for a promotion to captain during the following month. I looked him in the eye and told him that for two and one-half years I had been volunteering for overseas and was turned down. That I wasn't about to refuse now. To place my name on the list to go. I really believed that he was a weak leader, and put the monkey on my back. If he really wanted to promote me, he would have said nothing to me about the levy, promoted me the following month, and then sent me overseas. Well, at least I knew that I would be going now and help win the war.

The six of us proceeded by train to Ft. Shanks, New York where we were processed for overseas shipment. We were there for five days when we learned that we would be leaving from the Port of New York. It wasn't until we arrived at the harbor that we got the surprise of our life. We were going to sail on the *Queen Mary*, the world's largest and fastest liner! What a treat, we thought!

CHAPTER 10
Overseas on the Queen Mary

We departed on the twelfth of October 1944, and it wasn't too long after we got on board that we were all assigned extra duties. I was assigned to duties as packet commander, and given over two hundred men whom I was responsible to monitor during our Atlantic crossing.

The first order of the day after we set sail was that all packet commanders report to the main lounge. We were told to take along all the required documents and Allied papers. I asked my fellow officers what the Allied papers were? One of them said, "You don't have the Allied papers?" They were playing a trick on me, and I fell for it. I believed that the Allied papers were some foreign documents prepared by our Allies which pertained to our troops. Of course none existed, but every officer I asked gave me the question back as the first officer did. The word had gotten around and they were having their fun. I just suffered until all of us met in the grand lounge, and after going through the line with the documents I had, I found that I had them all. All my "friends" had their fun, and I learned a new meaning of the word.

The historical files of the *Queen Mary* revealed that on this trip there were 11,891 troops plus the crew aboard. The trip took five days, eight hours and 54 minutes from New York to Grenoch, Scotland. To say the least, we were one crowded boatload. The ship was divided into three compartments for administration. The divisions were made from top to bottom and were operated like three separate ships. The compartments were identified as red, white, and blue. The bow section was the red, the center, white, and the aft was called blue. I felt lucky in being in the white section since there should be less movement on the high seas. We were given badges with colors to match our assigned sections. No one was allowed to move about from one section to another.

All the officers, approximately two hundred of us, from the white section were assigned quarters on the starboard side of the promenade deck. Two hundred nurses, mostly lieutenants, were also assigned quarters on the promenade deck, but on the port side of the ship. Every one of us was so elated as to fall into such happy surroundings. We thought we were going to have a "Love Boat" atmosphere all the way over. How wrong we were! Guards were placed at each end of the nurses' passage way and no one was able to enter their quarters at any time or even remain around their hallway after hours.

My packet or company was quartered on "E" Deck which was some distance below the water mark. I didn't have much to do for the men's well-being except to visit their area several times a day, and see that all was going well. The first evening out, I really got a shocker when I was down visiting with my men and five o'clock rolled around. I heard a shrieking bell sound and then a voice giving some order. It meant that anyone not assigned to that deck had to leave. The reason being that all the doors leading to that compartment would be locked and would remain locked until daylight, the next morning. In case the ship was hit by a torpedo in that area during the night, only that compartment would be flooded, and the water would not travel to other parts of the ship. As I left the area and stood outside of those large compartment doors, I could see the discoloration in the men's faces and their anxiety, as the large doors squeaked to the locked position. What a feeling. To think that in case of a torpedo hitting that area, all of those men had to be sacrificed. I just didn't sleep well that first night, thinking of the men way down in "E" deck.

The days were taken up mostly by eating. We had two meals per day. One around eight or nine a.m., and the other around three or four p.m. It seemed that about the time we finished one meal it was time to line up for the next one. Our first morning out was my introduction to English "cuisine." We sat down for breakfast and the air was filled with a strong aroma of fish. We asked each other, "They wouldn't be serving fish for breakfast, would they?" All of us answered our own question, "No, they wouldn't." How wrong we were when soon came out their kippered herring and some other odds and ends. I tasted it, but didn't finish it. Then I watched my

The *Queen Mary* loaded with more than 12,000 troops on one of its many Atlantic crossings during World War II, October 1944.

Photo courtesy of the *Queen Mary* staff

friend from Texas, Captain John
Carter, receiving a pint bottle of whiskey under the table from one of the
stewards.

Even though there are regulations
against carrying liquor on board military ships, it seems that someone is
always able to get some aboard. I
couldn't stand the smell or looks of the
herring, so I left within minutes, and
went topside to get some air.

Commodore James Bisset, captain of *Queen Mary* during my
crossing of the Atlantic to Great
Britain, October 1944.

That evening all officers were ordered to go to the grand lounge to hear
the welcoming address by the ship's
captain, Commodore James Bisset,
who steered the *Queen Mary* on most

Photo courtesy
of the *Queen Mary* staff

of her crossings during World War II. All of us assembled around
seven p.m. Six or seven of us including Captain Carter sat around a
table in the right corner of the ball room and began telling jokes to
one another until the captain arrived. During this time I noticed
that Captain Carter had an extra happy face and was a little blush.
All of us wondered how he was getting his sipping. The secret was
soon out when he asked me to move over closer so he could whis-
per something into my ear. As I moved over I couldn't help but see
a long straw next to his necktie and coming out from inside his coat.
I leaned over, and he invited me to take a sip of his whiskey. He had
placed his bottle in the inside coat pocket and managed to telescope
several straws from the bottle up to the vicinity of his tie. We all
took turns at sipping and it wasn't long until all in our group were
"a little happier." Soon Commodore Bisset arrived and all gave him
a big hand. During his speech, he remarked that he was so delighted
that everyone was so happy, especially at our end of the room. I'm
sure he had our group in mind. He spoke only for a few minutes;
the assembly broke up, and all of us went our way.

During the next day, I got acquainted with one of the nurses
who was from Texas, and on board in the cabins next to ours. She

was a beautiful brunette with a figure to match, a true Southern Belle. We spent some time together on deck and talked about the war. That evening she asked me if I wouldn't take her topside to see the troops. During the nighttime, enough troops were brought topside and were permitted to sleep on deck. This allowed them to get some fresh air, and also get away from that horrible enclosure below deck. Each night a different deck of troops was allowed to rotate topside.

Shortly after dinner, the nurse and I met on deck and we started walking through the narrow opening left between the soldiers lying on deck. She asked me many questions, such as where the soldiers came from, and where we thought they were going. It soon became too much for her, when she saw the deck just solid with troops trying to get some sleep. She broke down crying. I tried to comfort her, by putting my arm around her. She finally stopped crying. I grasped her hand, and walked carefully back to our quarters. We promised to see each other the next day.

The next morning came and we completed the same breakfast routine, except this time I gained my strength, and was able to face

Commodore Bisset with his staff of the *Queen Mary*, during my crossing of the Atlantic to Great Britain, October 1944.

Photo courtesy of the *Queen Mary* staff

the herring again. This time I took just a bite or two and called it quits. During the day I walked the deck and when I arrived at the highest deck, I noticed a nice, small portico closed on three sides, and a canvas curtain across its front. It looked like a small storage area, but now it was empty. I thought it would be a nice place to bring my nurse friend and have a little privacy that evening. What a luxury this would be! A little privacy on such a crowded ship. When evening came, we met at the appointed place, and I again began escorting her through the narrow walkway.

Soon we reached the stairs which led up to another deck. Everywhere we walked there were soldiers. We soon came to another set of stairs and another deck. We were now as high as we could go. I started searching for our "private" room that I had discovered that afternoon. After more walking and weaving through the troops, I finally found our hideaway. I went and pulled the canvas curtain over, so that we could enter and I almost stumbled. What a shock and disappointment, the room which had been so empty and appealing that afternoon was now filled with soldiers sleeping on the deck inside. Well, I grasped my friend by the hand once again and slowly returned back to our deck. I realized now that, at least on this trip, the *Queen Mary* was not going to be a "Love Boat."

The remainder of the five-day trip was uneventful, but still always full of suspense. Since we had no escort vessels, or the like, one couldn't help have in back of his mind that on one of her trips even the *Queen Mary* could be hit by a lucky torpedo. On the 18th of October, we arrived in Scotland and landed at Grenoch, on the firth of Clyde, not too far from where the *Queen Mary* had been built. The ship had averaged 27.15 knots per hour on this trip. My first thoughts were that we were going to stay on board that night of arrival, and then leave first thing the next morning. I also was hoping that we would start debarking top deck first, and bottom deck last. None of my two expectations took place. First we started debarking as soon as we reached port, and secondly we began debarking bottom deck first. As it turned out, my packet on "E" deck was one of the first to debark. I accepted everything because we were in a war, but I did mind not seeing more of Scotland.

CHAPTER 11
The British Isles

W e rode by train through Scotland, Wales, England and finally reached Chester, in the south of England, where we were quartered for four days. The stark two story barracks weren't much for comfort. They contained simple cots and no heat. Worst of all a trough outside, similar to the ones I had seen in some western movies to water horses, provided our cold water, not only for washing, but also for shaving. I'm happy to say that our stay around Chester didn't last long.

Several of us officers did visit downtown, and had our first visit to a pub. We negotiated our way there by cab and then by walking. The city was completely blacked out and we didn't know where we were going. The cabby suggested this one pub, and so we took him up on it. It was quite a relief when we opened a door, and saw light. The smoke was thick and the place was full of native men putting a little of the old malt down. We ordered one ourselves, and to our amazement, when it arrived it was warm. I had heard about the English warm beer, but this was my first experience in trying to drink it. It was too much heat for me, so I waited and waited until it cooled off a bit, before I tackled it. After downing several of these, we decided we had enough. We hailed a cab and returned to the comforts of our camp and its cold water.

We remained around camp for several days and tried to keep clean and warm. Soon our orders came and we again entrained and headed south. Within a few hours we arrived at Southampton, and immediately boarded several landing crafts, tanks (LSTs), which were docked near the railhead. We remained in the harbor, almost until midnight, when we lifted anchor and headed for the coast of France.

CHAPTER 12
The Cherbourg Peninsula

After a rough overnight crossing of the English Channel we arrived at Omaha Beach on the coast of France. The ship moved as close to shore as possible. We came down by nets which were hanging over the sides, to where they had small landing boats waiting for us. All the men had to wait until the small boats came up as high as possible, and as close to the bottom of the nets as possible. They would then release their hold of the net and drop into the waiting boats. It was a very tricky maneuver, especially since none of us had any previous real experience with this procedure. The small boats then took us a bit closer to shore, until they reached long wooden causeways, on which we walked to shore. In all, we were relieved that we didn't have to make this same trip under fire on D-Day several months earlier.

As we slowly marched up those cliffs that had guarded the coast on the fateful D-Day, we could see the remnants still there, i.e., blown-out pillboxes, destroyed coastal guns, barbed wire, and hexagons, which had been used by the Germans to defend the coastline and beaches. I couldn't help recreate in my mind the beach landings that had been made by our men on D-Day, as I walked across the sand and climbed the hill to our bivouac area. I could almost sense the hurt our wounded men experienced as they struggled so gallantly and bravely to overcome the enemy. You could almost hear the sounds of gunfire in the crisp ocean air.

Our bivouac area was situated in an old apple orchard not far from Carenton on the Cherbourg Peninsula. Everyone pitched tents and tried to be comfortable for the two days we remained there. We could be called to strike tents and leave for the front at any time. One of the older officers, a lieutenant of maybe twenty-eight years of age, said that this area was known for its Calvados, the alcoholic drink made from apples. He then took off on foot to the nearby village, against all orders, to pick up a bottle of the potent drink. By late afternoon, a big rainstorm was threatening and he still had not returned to his little pup tent under an apple tree.

Just before it got dark, we saw a weaving shadow of a man approaching. He was holding a partially filled bottle and was having difficulty walking. As soon as he got closer we recognized him as the officer from our camp. He was really drunk, but managed to crawl into his tent, dragging his bottle with him. He fell asleep before his head touched the ground.

Soon, the raindrops began falling. It wasn't long before the entire orchard area was a quagmire. It didn't help much either when we went through the chow line, and all we were offered were hard-tacks (crackers) and coffee. When we complained to the lieutenant colonel in charge, he told us that our supply lines had broken down and that most everything was going to the front. We heard this excuse all the way until we reached the front lines. When we lacked any supplies on the front lines the excuse was reversed, and we were told that everything was being kept in the rear areas. Our morale was at rock bottom. I thought, how could this be? I hoped that the soldiers up front were feeling better than we were. The same menu was repeated for the next morning and lunch. By now we were almost ready to mutiny, but by the late afternoon, the long awaited supply of rations arrived. All were K-rations. This was not what we expected, but it was better than what we had been getting.

That evening our large units were broken down into smaller units of thirty-five to forty men each, with an officer in charge of each unit. I was assigned thirty-six men. By now the rain was really a downpour. Each of us officers tried to awaken our "Calvados Kid," without success. He was out cold.

We spent that night in our apple orchard villas, and when dawn broke we found ourselves with new orders to move. My men and I, along with most of the others in the camp, were ordered to march to the nearby railhead. As we walked by the tent where our drunken lieutenant lay, we all nudged him and pulled on his feet, trying to wake him up. He remained asleep, and that's the last time I saw him. All of us left the area. We arrived at the train station and boarded, putting all my men and myself in one of those cars similar to the "Forty and Eights" of World War I fame. They received their name for the forty men or eight horses they could carry. Before long we were on our way to the front, with about a five-day supply of K-rations. We made ourselves as comfortable as possible on the hard-wood floor, as our train began steaming away.

CHAPTER 13
Trip to the Front

Some twenty hours later we found ourselves in the heart of the Paris rail yards. From the moment we arrived until some twenty hours later we were put through the most trying test of patience possible. Every so often the train would shift back a few hundred yards, then forward the same or more distance, but on a different track. We thought this shifting would never end.

Sometime during midmorning of the following day, one of the officers from our train got off and was seen walking along the track next to the train. When asked where he was going, he said that he was going to see a little of Paris. He thought that our train would be shifting back and forth for another ten or twelve hours, and that the train would still be there when he planned to return. Well, it didn't happen that way. Within several hours, the train made its last shift and instead of stopping after it had moved a few yards forward, it kept going. Coincidentally we were hanging out of the large door on the side of our car and could see our AWOL officer running as fast as he could, trying to catch our train. To our disappointment, and I'm sure his, he never made it. All I remember is him running with arms stretched up in the air waving as if to tell the engineer to stop. That's the last time any of us saw that officer, too. We had not even entered combat, and we had already lost two officers.

We moved out slowly but steadily through Paris and all of us were thinking of a day when we could visit the city under better conditions. We rode all night. All of my men and I sat on the floor huddled against one another trying to keep warm. We tried to sleep, but every time we went into a sound sleep, we would be awakened by a sharp jolt of the train, either when it was slowing down for a curve or going through some village in the French countryside.

We arrived at Le Mans the next morning frozen stiff from the cold ride. The train was parked in the rail yard which had been previously bombed by the Allied Air Force. We were to remain there the rest of the day. The first thing everyone thought of was building a fire. Bon fires sprouted up all over the rail yard with groups of soldiers around each one of them. We were all rejoicing because we now had a fire and could warm up a bit. Everyone started making coffee and broke open their K-rations. Within minutes, this bit of happiness was cut short by the sound of an exploding shell at one of the fires. We ran over to see what had happened and saw a soldier on the ground with a wounded leg. He had been hit by a fragment from a shell that had exploded from under the fire. It dawned on us that, since the rail yard had been subjected to an air raid some weeks before, the shell had to be a dud from one of the twenty millimeter guns used during the raid. We immediately put all fires out and spent the rest of the day rubbing our hands together and walking around trying to keep warm. The wounded man was sent to a nearby hospital and soon we were on our way again. We had no idea where we were going or to what unit we were going to be assigned.

My men and I occupied one of the smallest 40 and 8 rail cars on the line. I guessed that was the way the cookie crumbled, so we boarded again, knowing that we could not get better reservations. We moved out slowly through the night air, and were getting colder by the minute. On one of the train's many stops, I asked the men to look for an old metal drum along the railroad. It wasn't long until we spotted one right next to the tracks, where we stopped. A couple of the men ran out quickly, picked it up and brought it back to our car. I immediately directed the job of making a stove. One end of the drum was cut out with our entrenching tools. Then holes were punched into the sides at the other end of the barrel, within six or so inches from the bottom. At last we had a stove! It was now nine or ten o'clock at night and getting colder by the minute.

The next job was to pick up some gravel or rocks from along the tracks, and place them in the middle of our car in a moundlike shape. This would serve as a base for our new stove. We did much of the work by feel, since it was pitch black by now and we couldn't see much of anything. We gathered our rocks during our next stop and our stove was ready for use, but now we needed fuel.

Our next stop wasn't too far away. We jumped, and took advantage of the opportunity by gathering wood and the like, so we could start our fire. Everyone was really full with anticipation knowing that we would soon be able to have some heat in our car. Most of the men were now huddled together seated on the floor and around the walls of the car. It was almost midnight by now and our choo-choo was moving along at a steadier speed. The men that helped put the stove together and I were pretty happy and satisfied at our accomplishment. We had a roaring fire within moments, and thought we would join the rest and try to get a little shuteye.

I sat down in the first row next to the stove and was able to feel considerable heat. After a couple of hours of half asleep and half awake, I smelled and saw smoke coming out from the bottom area of the barrel. I jumped up, awoke the men closest to our new heater, and began to search for the source of the smoke. To my shock, the stick that I used to poke around the base of the stove went right through the floor. I knew we had a problem. By now most of the men were awake and trying to help. The barrel was moved over to the big sliding door, which had been pulled open just enough to accommodate the barrel, and the barrel dumped out along the track. Our problem became bigger by the moment. Another look to where the barrel had been revealed that the "stones" that we had placed under the stove turned out to be coke, and were red hot. Upon shoveling the hot coke out the door, we discovered that the hot "stove" had burned a hole through the floor, and the floor was now on fire. Now would have been a great time for the train to make one of its many frequent stops, but it wasn't in the cards. It was now about two o'clock in the morning and the air was cold and crisp. The fire was whipping under the floor, and reminded me of one Wild West movie I once saw of a similar looking train running wild down the track on fire with Indians on horseback chasing it. Our train was moving faster by the minute, which encouraged the fire to exhort its ego to the maximum. My only option now was to awaken all the men, make a circle around the fire and do their duty. Our fire was finally out. The making of our stove was not completely successful, but we were able to get several hours of sleep. When we arrived at Liege, Belgium, our final train destination, the car, along with its charred hole was swept and cleaned out. I made sure that all the remaining empty large K-ration boxes were neatly stacked over the burned-out hole, so that the rail inspector could not see the damaged floor. The inspector soon came through and thought our

One of the many foxholes covered with logs for added protection against artillery fire. This one is similar to the one in which I spent my first night on the Belgian–German border. (November 1944)

car was very clean. I thanked him with tongue in cheek, knowing that we had passed inspection. I have always wondered whether France ever gave Uncle Sam a bill for the damaged car.

All of us were then trucked to a replacement depot in the vicinity of Verviers, Belgium, where we were broken up into smaller groups and sent to the front as replacements. Not much time was wasted here as I remember. It was now mid-November and getting colder by the hour. You could feel that winter was lurking around the corner. A driver with a jeep picked me up and delivered me to a place near the Belgian-German border named Losheimgraben. As I arrived, it began raining and intermittently snowing. It must have been raining for sometime prior to my arrival, since the entire area was full of puddles and mud. It looked so bad that I wondered how the vehicles were able to negotiate the roads and trails. By now it was around four p.m. and getting darker. The clouds were hanging low over the trees, and occasionally a streak of moist air would move down slowly as if wanting to touch the ground. It was almost fog. What welcoming weather. I was just introduced to the Ardennes. A runner met me at the headquarters of the 394th Infantry Regiment of the 99th Division and took me by jeep to the 3rd Battalion Command Post. The air was still heavy with moisture, and occasionally raindrops kept dropping from the tall fir trees that made up the dense forest.

I walked into a bunker made of logs that had been cut down in the vicinity. The bunker's log roof was covered with about a foot of dirt. One side of it had an opening, which served as the door, but was covered with a canvas curtain. This was the battalion headquarters. I entered, saluted, and reported to a lieutenant colonel, the battalion commanding officer. He was seated on a tall box next to a table which had a map on it. His face was flushed and the aroma of bourbon whiskey from his breath was overpowering. His first words to me were, "Lieutenant, there is the enemy out there." I thought to myself, what else could I expect? This was a war zone. He then told me that he was going to assign me to Company I, which

Spot on the Siegfried Line, Belgian–German border, where the Battle of the Bulge began for our 99th Division.

was on the front line and down the road a piece. He almost fell off his seat as he was trying to talk to me. I learned later that I was the last officer he assigned, for he was relieved of his command that same evening and reassigned back to the States.

He ordered me to report to my Company I, right away. I saluted him and walked out. A runner was waiting for me outside. He took me through the forest up to a road which led parallel to the front line. We crossed this road and could hear intermittent machine gun fire coming from a long distance to the East. It was still awful wet and muddy out. We went about fifty yards and took what appeared to be a logging trail through another fir forest. The trail was so muddy that logs had been laid across for long stretches, so that jeeps and other vehicles could travel over it. This was the Belgian-German border area.

CHAPTER 14
Assignment to Combat Unit

W e finally arrived at the Company I Command Post (CP) and I reported in to Captain James J. "J.J." Morris from San Francisco. The CP was a large tent used for supplies and clerical work. This was surrounded by a series of bunkers built out of local logs, and half buried underground. I knew I had reached the front lines.

We sat down on a couple of K-ration boxes. Captain Morris told me that the company was short of officers, and that I would be assigned to two duties. My primary being that of executive officer for the company, and secondary, that of platoon leader of the second platoon. After talking about our families and homes, we bedded down for the night in the bunkers. I was amazed how quiet the battle front was. Only once in a great while the stillness of the night was broken by some sporadic rifle fire or machine gun fire in the distance, probably from patrol activities. I was now resigned to the fact that I was going to be fighting for my country and help end the war in a hurry.

After breakfast the next day, Captain Morris took me on an orientation tour of the company front. We started walking and were going to cover only the right half of the company front that day. We were to tour the left half on the following day. To my surprise the foxholes in some cases were located two hundred to three hundred feet apart. The man in one foxhole could not see the man in the next one. I asked Captain Morris why so much distance between holes, and that it would be very difficult to defend our position in case of an attack. He replied, "Forget what they taught you at Benning. This is the way they told us to do it over here." The division was stretched to over twenty miles instead of the normal seven to eight miles, so likewise, the company was also stretched beyond what it could normally defend.

After spending two days just visiting our rifle company front, I knew that we were stretched. I just couldn't believe it. The next day, as promised, Captain Morris and I visited the left half of our front. I just couldn't stop thinking that any German patrol wanting to come through could do it without any difficulties. In some areas the terrain was so rough and the trees so thick, that no one could be seen, let alone the enemy. This was the latter part of November 1944, and I had just completed my first two weeks on the front line. I now felt I was a veteran.

On the 30th of November, I was given an additional assignment, that of paymaster. It was not a too demanding duty back in the States, but here it was different. Not only did I have to pay the men on the Main Line of Resistance (MLR), but also those few out at the Outpost Line of Resistance (OPLR).

While paying the men occupying the foxholes on the MLR was not too bad even though they were widely separated, the ones on the OPLR were another story. They were really out in front, possibly a thousand yards, and were to act as scouts for the MLR. In other words, they were the eyes and ears for the front line. In case of attack, the OPLR would be hit first and thereby the MLR would be alerted in time to prepare for a better defense.

Little did I know how complex this assignment was going to be. I was accompanied by a jeep driver, who also assisted me in paying our men. I had picked up the payroll which was in military script in Verviers, and proceeded back to the front. It was raining a cold rain, half water and half snow. After struggling through poor roads and numerous convoys of trucks we made it back to our area. Upon our arrival at the company CP, we had some hot coffee and braced ourselves for the job ahead. I soon realized what I was faced with. I paid the soldier in script, he in turn handed back most of it to have a money order made out for him. Most of the men also had English pounds and French and Belgian francs for exchanging into military script. They had picked up these monies on their way from the States. This was their first payday on the front line.

It took me the rest of the day, and the morning of the next day to finish the job. When I got through with all the transactions, I had 562 French francs left. I felt lucky at that, not having more left over in my bag. I turned the francs over to the finance officer in Verviers, along with the "not paid" note for the 562 francs. He was amused, but almost with a reprimanding tone in his voice, asked, "Why didn't you keep the francs instead of ruining our books?" I got a receipt and left with a sigh of relief and a clear conscience.

All went well along the front during the next two weeks, with very little action seen by anyone. In fact, it was too quiet. Once in awhile we would hear the sound of rifle fire here and there in the distance, accompanied by a small burst of machine gun fire. The accepted reason for the disturbance was always, "It's only patrol activity."

Every late afternoon small patrols made up of one officer, usually a lieutenant, and five or six men would walk by our supply tent, and head toward the front. They would follow the trail that cut through the tall forest of trees and led right into the German lines. It wouldn't be long until we would hear an explosion. Within a half hour or so the patrol would be walking back, carrying one of their wounded. The wound was always the result of stepping on a mine. The mines which made up the large mine fields on the Belgian-German border were now covered by snow, therefore presenting a much more hazardous situation. Patrols of this nature continued through mid-December 1944.

On the 15th of December, 1944, our company was pulled back from the font line and moved to an assembly area several miles to the rear. The area was called Losheim. Some log cabins had been built by some other company previous to our arrival, and some were in different stages of completion. It was a nice place to get a little rest, and also to continue on the project of finishing all the cabins. We packed all our supplies in one of the cabins, and then began enjoying our rest. Our company was now designated as the Regimental Reserve. While there, I went through my duffel bag to make sure my white dress uniform was still there. It was there, and again I imagined how soon I would be going to the Riviera and wear it. Everyone laughed when they saw my white uniform and doubted that I would ever get to use it. No one could imagine why anyone would bring a white uniform to a cold and freezing area like the Ardennes. Our rest lasted only twenty-four hours. On the next day, the 16th of December, the German army decided to start one of the biggest attacks of the war, later to be known as the Battle of the Bulge.

In the late afternoon of December 16th, our company was ordered to move out. Our mission was to make contact with, and assist the 3rd Battalion of the 393rd Regiment of our division. We moved out, after securing our supply cabin, along a logging trail in the middle of a tall thick fir forest. We followed the trail known as Schwarzenbruch in two files, one on each shoulder of the trail. We soon arrived at the headquarters of the 393rd Regiment which was located in an old country house on our left, next to the road. Captain Morris stopped the company along the road next to the house and sent me into the headquarters to receive our orders.

Upon entering, I saw four or five officers and several men scurrying around almost in a state of confusion. I saluted and reported to a captain who was the S-3 (operations officer), and he put me at ease, by having me walk over to a map on the wall. There were also several other lieutenants studying the map. The S-3 began briefing me on the situation, which at best was very marginal. Basically, he told me that they had lost contact with their 3rd Battalion during that morning, and that all efforts to regain contact had failed. It was believed that a patrol in force, possibly fifty men or more, had broken through our lines, and had destroyed our communications.

Company I's mission was to move up to the 3rd Battalion area and re-establish contact with their 3rd Battalion headquarters under command of Lieutenant Colonel Allen. I studied the map so that I could get a good idea where the battalion was located. I then saluted and began walking out the door. The door was only half-opened when I was called back, and at the same time, I overheard one of the lieutenants say, "You better give him a secondary order." When I faced the S-3 again, he said, "We thought you better have a secondary order. After you establish contact with the battalion, restore the MLR." This was a tall order, if things were really in bad shape at the front. I saluted again, departed and joined my awaiting company along the road.

I showed Captain Morris my map, passed on the orders which I had just received and we resumed our march towards the front. A column of widely separated men walked along each side of the road, each man to his own thoughts not knowing what was in store for us. We walked over a gradual rise in the landscape and started down a small hill and into the thick forest. The trail was getting narrower and darker as we got closer to the front.

CHAPTER 15
Battle of the Bulge

Afterter walking several hundred yards into the forest, we met our first encounter with enemy fire. We heard screaming artillery shells coming from the direction of the front, and over the trees. At first, a chill went down my back, since I had never heard such sounds before, and didn't know what they were. I yelled to all the men around me to hit the dirt. Within seconds, a second volley screamed overhead! The shells hit the top of the trees and exploded. All of us were flat on the ground trying to wrap ourselves deeper with the earth. Luckily, no one in my platoon was hit.

No more shells were heard for the moment. Soon word came back through the line from Captain Morris that the shells were German 88's. I was also informed from the rear that one man had been slightly wounded by the flying shrapnel, and was evacuated. We continued walking down the small hill, which soon gave way to a lesser grade and then a flat area. The flat area was also devoid of trees, and looked no different than an open campground site in the middle of a state park back in the States. A message came back from Captain Morris, who was leading the column, that contact had been made with Colonel Allen, CO of the 3rd Battalion, and that we were to dig in for the night.

I placed my platoon in a semicircle around the edge of the open area and on top of a bank. The bank which sloped to the rear led

down to a small stream bed. All of us began digging in and continued through the early evening hours until each of us had our own
foxhole. I was situated on the highest ground and near a large tree.
To my disappointment, halfway through my digging, I ran into a
very large root and could not go any deeper. I guess it didn't matter
much, since I remained awake throughout the entire night anyway.
All through the night we could hear noises, like that of an owl or
animal. I told my men that the noises were probably made by German patrols, trying to ferret out our positions. I ordered everyone
to remain very quiet after they were dug in. The night passed without encountering any further enemy action.

The morning came and there still seemed to be a lot of confusion around the area. I tried to obtain some information as to what
was going on from Captain Morris, but he also was not receiving

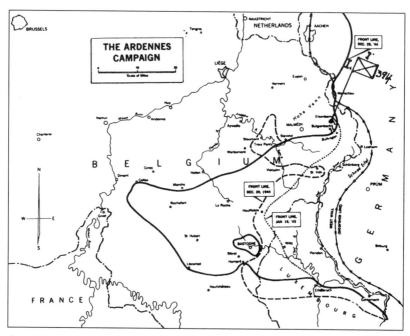

General map of the "Battle of the Bulge" campaign. Bottom of flag staff shows
general location of our 99th Division which held the northern shoulder of
Elsenborn Ridge, and helped to change the course of the battle.

Photo courtesy of the Department of Defense

much input. I was getting restless, so I walked over to the Aid Station which was located maybe a hundred feet from me, at the opposite edge of the clearing. There was a 3/4-ton truck waiting and a captain (the medical officer) was running around and busylike. He was trying to see which patients could be moved by this one last trip, by the truck, and which were to stay and surrender. He had made the decision to remain with the latter group. It wasn't until this very moment that I realized how serious the situation was. I now heard the battalion was facing one *Panzer* and two *Volksgranadier* Divisions. That's almost fifty thousand men and hundreds of tanks.

I then looked down at the ground next to the tent, and saw an opened box half full of Hershey chocolate bars. I asked the captain what he was going to do with them and he replied, "Nothing", and that I could have them. We could hear increased rifle and machine gun fire at a distance and an occasional round of artillery, whining over the trees, but no action where I was, except the scurrying around by the personnel near the Aid Station.

To break the boredom and try to raise morale, I took the opened box of candy and, starting at one end of the line, carried the box at waist height, walking and announcing, "Chocolates, Chocolates." Most of the men were very serious by now. I'm sure the status of the situation had just sunk in. They took the chocolate bars, but I could not get a smile from anyone. I tried to raise their morale and hope I did so, even if it didn't show in their faces. This was the only good candy they had seen for a long time, I'm sure. The

Lyle J. Bouck, Jr., commanded I&R Platoon, 394th Regiment on 16 December 1944. He was responsible for stopping the German 6th *Panzer* Army near Lanzerath, Belgium, which was being spearheaded by SS Colonel Joachim Peiper, Germany's "Hot Shot." Lieutenant Bouck's heroic action delayed the German Grand Plan for eighteen hours and caused them to divert some of their actions from Elsenborn Ridge to Bastogne. Lieutenant Bouck was awarded the Distinguished Service Cross for his extraordinary heroism.

Photo courtesy of the Department of Defense

Joachim Peiper, German SS colonel, spearheaded the main thrust of the 6th *Panzer* Army on 16 December 1944, and was stopped near Lanzerath by our 394th I&R Platoon, commanded by Lieutenant Lyle J. Bouck, Jr. Even though he was Germany's best he was delayed some eighteen hours, had to turn around and re-route his attack.

Photo courtesy of the Department of Defense

chocolate candy contained in our K-rations was a long way from Hershey bars.

This was now mid-morning of the 17th of December and the situation was deteriorating by the moment. I thought maybe we could carry some of the wounded men back with us, but were told that they were too badly wounded to move. Finally, Captain Morris came to my platoon area and informed me that we had orders to move back the best way we could and establish a defense line near Elsenborn. The captain and I looked over the map and hopefully selected the best route back away from the Germans. I knew that if we remained to our right rather than our left we might evade any enemy infiltrators along the way. The trail we took was bounded by a forest on our left side. There was an open draw to our right with a small stream, then a bank, another open field, and then a thick forest up on the hillside.

We began our long march back, not knowing whether or not the Germans would attack our column before we reached our final destination, Elsenborn. Periodically, I looked back to see if any of the enemy was on our trail. To our relief, none was. This relief didn't last long though. I could hear the rumbling of tanks, somewhere in the forest, to our left rear. I had everyone go down into the draw and remain still. I laid low near the top of the embankment, and kept looking towards the woods where the noise was coming from. Soon a tank appeared from a trail at a right angle to the trail we were on, and at a point we had just passed. I was hoping for a long shot, that they were our tanks. As they emerged from the forest trail, I could see two of them, and both had the cross markings on them.

They were German Mark V tanks. My heart went to my throat during the next moment. I was asking myself, "Are they going to turn right and away from us, or left and be on top of us?" Was I relieved when both of them made a right turn towards the area from which we had just left. The men still remained low and out of sight. When the tanks were out of my sight, I waved to the men that all was clear. Much relieved, we continued our march to the rear. What a close call! I'm sure we would have been put to our test if the tanks had turned towards our position, but I was happier the way it turned out. We kept bearing to the right as we moved to the rear. I had a feeling of being compressed into a funnel as we got closer to our destination. The farther we walked, the more congested the roads became. Just before darkness fell on us, we met other men of the 394th Regiment and personnel of the 2nd Infantry Division. Trucks, artillery pieces, etc. were stuck in the mud in the fields along our route, apparently abandoned. It was now beginning to sink in that the situation was very serious. Thoughts went through my mind that we must hold at some point, and not let Hitler win this war. America just must not lose!

Gun position on Elsenborn Ridge.

Photo courtesy of the Department of Defense

Remnants of pillbox used for my platoon headquarters on Elsenborn Ridge during the Battle of the Bulge. Looking east into Germany, edge of woods was the front line of the German army. (50 years later, 1994)

We were able to arrive at some high ground past Murrigen, at which point we stopped and were told to dig in. The field, lined on its borders by small hedge rows, common to the Belgian country-side, had piles of large beets here and there. Since we had not eaten since the morning of the sixteenth, everyone was starved. I thought the beets were for the farmer's cattle, and as such they should be edible. So, I cut one with my bayonet, took a sliver and took a bite. I told my men that if I didn't get sick within minutes, and jokingly, if I didn't die, they could go ahead and eat them too. A few minutes went by and nothing happened. A few of the men were brave enough to try them, but the beets were so hard and stringy that they were no "gourmet delight." After chewing through one slice, we called it quits. That small interlude at least took our minds off the battle that was raging around us.

We formed a line on the hillside, but I don't remember much digging taking place, since this was only an interim stop on the way to our final destination. As everyone looked back to the south and southwest, we could see fires raging in the towns that lay before us, such as Krinkelt-Rocherath and Wirtzfeld. After an entire night of waiting, not knowing what was coming up next, we continued towards Elsenborn. On the way, as dawn was breaking, an enemy plane was seen coming over the horizon and strafing our troops along the road. All of us hit the dirt on each side of the road. The roar rushed over our heads, with machine guns spitting out their bullets into the ground around us. Luckily none of us was hit. This

American soldiers massacred by SS Colonel Peiper's men near Malmedy, Belgium. I saw the bodies during a special trip to Malmedy and could not believe my eyes. (circa 15 January 1945)

Photo courtesy of the Department of Defense

was the only strafing my men and I encountered during the war. By mid-afternoon we arrived at our destination, the Elsenborn Ridge. A line of defense was designated and everyone was ordered to dig in.

Panther tank (Mark V), same model of which I saw two traveling towards our company during our route to Elsenborn Ridge. We were much relieved when the tanks turned away from us when they were 300–400 yards away.

Photo courtesy of the Department of Defense

CHAPTER 16
On Elsenborn Ridge

The men were really hungry by now. The taste of beets didn't do much to pacify their hunger. I approached Captain Morris and asked him if I could take off to the rear and try to locate our kitchen. After some hesitation, he said that I could, and so my long trek through the snow started. As I looked back to the west, I could see the spire of the church at Elsenborn on the horizon. It appeared to be several miles away. It was my aiming point. As I struggled through the thick snow across a large open field, I could see a plane right above the tree tops, coming directly in my direction. I thought it was one of ours, so I waved. To my shock and embarrassment, it turned out to be an enemy plane. As it flew directly over me, the *Luftwaffe* markings under the wings shot out at me like two bright lights. It was a Folke-Wolfe 190. Within a split second, one of our planes, a P-47, swooshed right behind him in pursuit. I watched them climbing higher and higher, with the P-47 closing in for the kill. He let a burst of gunfire go and the enemy plane burst into fire and smoke. Our plane veered off to the right and into the open sky. The enemy plane went into a climb, stalled, and right at that moment, the pilot bailed out. The plane made a nose dive in flames. The pilot floated down in his parachute, at some distance away. I learned later that he was captured by our troops south of Elsenborn. This was the only dog fight I have ever seen, and reminiscent of the air-battles of World War I that I had seen in movies back home.

I continued walking through the snow-carpeted field towards the church spire and, possibly, food. I arrived at the church before dark, and began searching and inquiring among all the personnel that were squeezed into the narrow streets. It wasn't long until I saw a face I recognized. It was that of our cook, Sergeant Demperio. We ran towards each other, and violated all rules against familiarity between officers and enlisted men, and followed our instincts. We embraced and exchanged a few words. He was so happy to see me and I him. He wanted to know where the company was, and told me that they tried to contact us since the 16th of December, and no one seemed to know where we were. He wanted to know what kind of food and how much food we wanted. We filled the trailer with boxes of C and K-rations and took off to the front line. We hadn't traveled even a half mile on a narrow farm road when we heard incoming artillery exploding in front of us. The sergeant stopped the jeep, and we both jumped out for cover. One shell hit pretty close and splattered mud on the jeep and trailer, but we escaped without a scratch. We soon arrived at our company's area just as darkness fell and were greeted by several hundred hungry men. Everyone grabbed a K or C-ration, and it wasn't long until all had their tummies filled. It was now pitch black, but Sergeant Demperio had to return to the Elsenborn and his kitchen. We guided him to the road, headed him in the right direction and he departed.

That night, Captain Morris and I dug and dug and dug our foxhole. He and I were to share one. He wondered how deep we were going when we went past the normal depth for a foxhole. I said we ought to go as deep as we could. Soon we found ourselves some seven feet down. I had to dig steps into the end wall so that we could get in and out. By noon of the next day everyone was dug into their positions. All had plenty of rations, a place to stay, enemy action had subsided, and were quite content.

Just before dark, we saw our first close-up of enemy soldiers. Several German soldiers carrying a white flag with a red cross on it moved across our front, some three hundred feet away down the hill. They went left across our entire front and then right and disappeared towards their lines. Sgt. John D. Morris insisted that we should shoot at them. He thought that they were not aidmen looking for their wounded, but a reconnaissance patrol feeling our front. I told him I thought the same, since there hadn't been any shooting at this location yet, but as long as a red cross flag was being displayed, we would honor it and not fire. After all, there had been no fighting in the area, so how could they have any wounded to find. All agreed it was a reconnaissance patrol.

About an hour or so went by when all hell broke loose. The skies from the German side opened up with the largest artillery barrage we had encountered to date. Besides 88's and other heavy artillery, we received fire from *Nebelwerfer* Rocket batteries. They screamed through the air from their launchers with a shrill sound never heard before. It felt like the entire sky was falling in on us. Captain Morris lay down at the bottom of our hole at one end, and I at the other. Soon, we sustained a direct hit against the front parapet of our foxhole. The inside of our wall caved in on top of us. Captain Morris asked, "Sam, are you okay?" I replied, "Yes," and followed up with, "Are you okay?" After we were

Nebelwerfer Rocket gun used against our position on Elsenborn Ridge. Noted for creating the scariest noise of the war.

Photo courtesy of the Department of Defense

assured that we didn't sustain any wounds, we shook the dirt from on top of us and waited for the bombardment to cease. We thought that it would never stop. The incoming shell had hit the large pile of dirt in front of our hole. It's a good thing that we had dug down to seven feet. The large pile of dirt in front of our foxhole had saved our lives.

The shelling soon stopped. We were now bracing ourselves for some infantry charge up our hill. Within minutes, instead of that, we heard our own artillery responding. Some twenty-two battalions of artillery, I learned later, were engaged in this barrage. It was, by far, greater than what we had just received from the Germans. It lasted almost a half hour, and we couldn't be happier. I believe this barrage broke the enemy's back on the northern shoulder of the Bulge, and it never recovered. We waited for an attack, but it never came.

The line was now stable, and was shaken only by an occasional burst of artillery shells. I felt that after withstanding the initial barrage, we could take anything. The snow got deeper by the day and we settled down to keeping a strong defense posture and engaging in patrol activities.

German 88-MM Gun — Rated as the most accurate gun of the war. Model of gun that made a direct hit on our foxhole during the biggest bombardment that we had experienced. Hit caused the inside of the foxhole to cave in on Captain Morris and me. No injuries. Digging our hole seven feet deep paid off. I still kneeled and prayed to the Lord during the entire bombardment.

Photo courtesy of the Department of Defense

The word came through the field telephone that General Patton stated that "The Germans put their head in the meat grinder and he was coming up to turn the handle." I was to relate this message to every man in my platoon. I went around to each foxhole after darkness and repeated the message to each and every man. I don't know if this was the truth or just a ploy to boost the morale. I'm not sure if everyone accepted it as the truth, but I think that it did boost morale. At that moment, I believe, we would have believed anything that was favorable to us. Any movement on this ridge had to be done at night, otherwise we subjected ourselves to sniper fire from the valley below, and also artillery fire from the hills beyond.

The cold weather was taking its toll all along the front, mainly from trench foot. Cause of this ailment is lack of circulation, eventually causing gangrene to set in, and finally requiring amputation. In order to minimize this tragedy, I had all the men, who were now two per foxhole, take turns and walk through the platoon area back and forth for one half hour each night. Walking over an area many times hardened the surface, and because of the coldness it froze and became iced. Walking became extremely difficult, so we had to break a new path in the snow each time we went out. The program helped a lot, and I felt very lucky, since I lost only two men to trench foot. Both were then evacuated. One of them, Private Dallas, wrote me from England several weeks after he was evacuated and thanked me for ordering him to leave. He was so grateful that we caught his condition in time. His letter stated that when he entered the hospital in England, he was placed in a bed between two other soldiers suffering from the same ailment. The difference being, one had already lost one foot, and the other had both feet amputated. He felt so lucky that he saved both of his feet. I never heard from my second man. This was *our* Valley Forge.

We were continuing to receive our liquor and cigarette rations. I made use of the whiskey, with a little nip every night, but I saved all my cigarettes since I didn't smoke. I was looking forward to a future R & R in Paris or the Riviera and anticipating using the tobacco for bartering.

Once our front line was well stabilized, we learned that the German army had gone through and captured all our supplies during the initial days of the Bulge. Their route took them right to the cabins which we helped build at Losheim. I couldn't help imagining that some German officer, or soldier, found my white uniform and was prancing around their midst, with part of it on, and joking about some crazy American taking a white summer uniform to the Ardennes. Little did they know what my plans were. Oh, well, my vacation to the Riviera was just canceled.

The Ridge at Elsenborn was devoid of any trees, and thereby gave us a clear view down the hill, to the edge of the forest and the enemy. It also had some disadvantages, since every move we made was picked up by the Germans and was quickly followed by sniper fire. Right in front of their forest was a small stream, according to the map, but not visible now, due to the heavy snows that covered it. The condition gave us the advantage for defense, because of the high ground, but it favored the Germans for movement. The forest was so thick that it allowed them to move about at will, without interference from our side. Once in a great while, we would throw several rounds of artillery at their general area just to shake them up a bit, and to let them know that we were still around and watching them.

Because of the prevailing conditions, all patrols were conducted during nighttime. All companies along our front took turns at this activity, starting from our 1st Battalion, which was occupying the area to our right and followed by 2nd Battalion, and finally us. One night at about 2 a.m., my platoon sergeant Isadore Rosen, came and woke me up. He had another man with him. It turned out to be a sergeant from Company E of our 2nd Battalion. The Company E sergeant was very excited, talking very fast, asking for help. When I slowed him down a bit to see what the problem was, he told us that his lieutenant, or patrol leader, had been hit by machine gun fire, right in front of the German lines by the edge of the forest down the hill. There were six or seven men on the patrol from Company E. The rest of the men scattered and hopefully were back to our lines safely—the lieutenant was still alive, but unconscious. The sergeant wanted help to get his patrol leader out. He came to the nearest unit on the line.

I called Captain Morris on the walky-talky and asked if I could take a couple of my men and go down the hill on this rescue mission. I had to argue a bit, since the patrol was not from our company or even battalion. My justification was that Company E was too far away and it was now two a.m. If someone didn't go down there immediately, the rescue would not succeed. If we waited any longer, by the time we walked down there in the heavy snows and returned, daylight would be upon us before we reached our lines. We would then be at the mercy of the enemy fire, either machine gun or sniper. Captain Morris agreed with my reasoning. I took one rifleman and my medic, PFC John "Smoky" Marcisin from Connecticut, who carried the stretcher. Marcisin was given the nickname "Smoky" because he was the first person to build a fire, when it was safe to do so.

The sergeant from Company E led the way, with us following his footsteps down to the bottom of the hill, almost to the stream. We finally came up to the wounded officer, who was unconscious, but still warm and alive. The medic gave him a shot of morphine to help relieve any pain he surely must have been having. I had instructed the team that we could do no talking while in the vicinity of the German line. I was afraid that if the enemy heard any noise whatsoever, they might open up with their machine guns, just as a safeguard, and we may end up as casualties, too. Everyone did really well, and soon all our signals were by touch and motion. "Smoky" laid the litter down next to the officer, who weighed around 180-200 pounds. We rolled him over onto the litter and started back to our lines. We didn't hear any noises from the German side and hopefully we didn't make any ourselves. I have always wondered whether the Germans knew we were evacuating our wounded and didn't shoot, or that they couldn't see or hear us. At any rate, we began our exodus.

A snowstorm was now brewing. The flakes were heavy and the wind was changing every second, swirling the snow in every which direction. We didn't realize how difficult it was to move our man, until we lifted him. I had a feeling that everything was against us. The officer was heavy, the snow was at least two feet deep, our walk was all up a steep hill, and we were operating under war time conditions. The only thing in our favor was the darkness. I knew that with perseverance, we would make it.

We struggled up the hill in a general direction of our line. Our old tracks were already covered by the blowing snow, and we could not see much farther than a few feet ahead of us. I knew direction-wise that we would be all right, as long as we climbed. It was so difficult to walk that we tired out very easily. We had to stop and rest every several minutes. It seemed like eternity until we were out of the immediate enemy area. We still had an hour and a half or so of darkness, so I felt we were okay. After what seemed like the entire night, we arrived near our front line on top of the hill. To my amazement, I looked down where I was leading and the most unbelievable sight shot before my eyes. We were standing right at the opening of the barbed wire defenses. This was the exact spot from which we had started on our rescue mission, and probably the only opening for hundreds of yards in either direction. I looked up into the heavens and just knew we must have had divine guidance. Almost immediately someone on the line challenged us. I replied with our countersign for the day, and we were allowed to continue.

The dawn was now approaching, but one couldn't tell much, because of the gloomy snowstorm. Just several hundred feet and we were in our company area. I called for help to move the wounded officer back to our Aid Station. Our energies had been all but expended. I had a great sense of satisfaction that we had made it back before daylight. Within the hour, this euphoria was dampened by the news that the officer whom we tried so hard to save, had died at the Aid Station.

Our patrolling activity continued throughout the next several weeks. Finally it was my turn to go. Captain Morris called me to his dugout and told me that headquarters was needing POWs for interrogation. They were interested in knowing what troops we were facing, strength, type, etc. I was to take five men and conduct the patrol that night in early January.

The weather was still cloudy, stormy and cold. I picked my five men, and we got our gear together. I oriented them as to where we were going and the purpose of our mission. We started walking down the hill very carefully, as soon as darkness fell. Within the hour or so we were down by the stream bed in front of us. I had no information as to the locations already known, of bunkers, headquarters, and actual location of the enemy. I had to feel my way. This was as much a reconnaissance as a POW capturing patrol. By the time we arrived at the woods' edge a snowstorm had whipped up. We could not see ten feet ahead of us. As we started to enter the woods, I stepped into what must have been an old foxhole. It was covered with snow which was even with the rest of the ground around it, so there was no way to tell that it was there. Stepping into it was no problem, except that the bottom had six to eight inches of water in it. Besides being cold, it didn't bother me too much. Within minutes one of my men claimed that he was snow blind and could not see at all. The blinding snow was bad enough for the rest of us, so I could appreciate his predicament. I had to assign one of the other men to hold and guide him. By now my right foot, once exposed to the cold open air, began freezing. My pant leg was already stiff as cardboard. We could not see, because of the blowing snow; I had two men occupied with each other and I with a frozen foot. I knew that without a definite target such as a CP, or bunker, we would have to be lucky and accidentally bump into some German in order to capture him. Not having a target was bad enough, but worse was not being able to see one. I had to make a difficult decision, and I made it. I aborted the patrol and signaled the men that we were going back to our line. We struggled up the hill, one by one in another blowing snowstorm similar to the one several nights earlier when we went on our rescue mission. We reached the top of the ridge and found ourselves at the end of our company front. We were challenged, permitted to pass, and by midnight we were back in our own company area. I reported to Captain Morris and told him what a failure and disappointment my mission had been.

By now my right foot was feeling like a piece of wood and I knew it was frostbitten. "J.J." told me to go back to the Aid Station so that they could take care of it. At that time this was justification for receiving a Purple Heart. The same thing had happened to me previously in Pennsylvania when I was growing up so I knew what to do. Although my earlier incident was not half as bad as this one, the treatment was the same. I had read somewhere that you must pack snow around a frozen foot and it will soon thaw out. The only warning was not to rub the snow against the affected areas because it would have an adverse effect on it. So I sat next to my foxhole the rest of the night, and kept packing snow around my foot. I kept this up until ten or eleven o'clock the next morning, by which time I was suffering from extreme hot, burning pain. Even though in pain, I knew I was cured, since now I again had feeling in my foot.

Things went on about as routinely as one could expect on the battlefield in the middle of winter. A small break came near the end of January 1945, and I was given a twenty-four-hour pass to go to Verviers, Belgium, some twenty miles behind the lines. I was so happy that I could clean up a bit and thaw out. I arrived at our rest hotel, and it was time for chow. A hot meal was served, and what a treat! This was my first hot meal in over a month. I then made a beeline for the showers. I took my field clothes off and I believe they were almost able to stand up by themselves, almost like they were frozen stiff. I was issued a change of clothing and went straight into that hot shower. Never in my life did I believe that a hot shower could be so satisfying. After a good hot soaking, I felt that I was thawed out. I then went straight up to my room, got into my bunk, and that's all she wrote. I conked out and slept through until ten or eleven o'clock the next day.

I must have been totally exhausted, because never in my life had I ever slept more than five or six hours straight through. Just being back from the front line was a great relief in itself, adding a hot meal and a hot shower was just the epitome of life, I thought.

During the afternoon a Lieutenant Duncan, who was also back there for a rest, but from some other unit, and I decided to go for a walk and find a barber shop. We walked for several blocks up an inclined street that had a trolley line on it. After some searching we found our shop and went in. We didn't have to say anything, they could see we needed a haircut. There were two chairs, one operated by a man and one by a woman, the first female barber I had ever seen. Maybe we had some in the States, but I had just never seen one. The unusual thing about this was not that she was a woman barber, but that she held her scissors with both hands. Her right thumb and right forefinger holding one-half of the scissors around the hole and the left hand holding the left half. Duncan sat in the man's chair and I reluctantly sat in the woman's chair. We believed that they were a man and wife team. I kept looking in the mirror to see how she managed those scissors, but when she got through she had given me a good haircut. Neither of them spoke any English. We held out some Belgique francs, they took what was the price, and we were on our way.

We then crossed the street, and saw what had been an old restaurant, but now closed. We knocked on the door and soon an elderly short man came to the door. We motioned to our mouths, indicating that we wanted to eat. He let us enter, and we sat at a small table for two, near the window. He pulled up a chair and joined us. He didn't speak any English either, but we got along fine. This was just a social visit at first. We took turns looking at photos of our families, etc. Then, I told him we wanted beef steak; he hesitated, but I believe he understood. He then took off down the street and soon returned with two good looking, but very lean steaks, the likes of which I had never seen. In the meantime, we were all alone, Lieutenant Duncan and I. The old restaurant was totally deserted and inactive.

I then told the old gentleman that I was going to cook the beef myself and needed some oil. He didn't understand, then he said, *"le beurre"* — it sounded like butter, so we replied, "Oui! Oui!" He again disappeared down the street and, in minutes, he returned with what looked like about two tablespoons of butter. He then lit a fire in an old cook stove in the alcove next to where we were sitting. We finally were going to have an old American steak. I couldn't wait until the fire got hot enough to cook. When the time arrived, I placed the butter in a large frying pan that the old man provided, and began frying it. This was far from a barbecue, but we had a steak. The old man was so curious that he kept watching everything I did with the steaks. I had no expertise in Belgian cooking, but I wondered if he ever cooked a steak this way. When the steaks were done, he gave us knives, forks and two plates. We served ourselves, sat at our table, and began eating. I offered the old man a taste, but he wouldn't have any of it.

We thought that we were on top of the world when we were finished with our steaks. We held some francs out, he took what he wanted, and we were on our way back to the Rest Center. There, Lieutenant Duncan went his way and I got on a $2^1/_2$-ton truck, and with some twenty other officers we returned to the front. It was a great twenty-four hours. Later on, I was informed that what we had eaten was probably horse meat. The Belgians had run out of beef because of the war and were serving only horse meat by now. No wonder the steaks were so lean. Well, anyway, it served the moment and it was too late now to change it. We had had our steaks.

We were now into late January, and we received orders to move and take new positions to our left several miles. The snow was still deep, which made walking laborious. We were still visible to the enemy, on top of the ridge, so we traveled a little behind the crest so that we could not be seen. When we came to my designated area, we found a large mound of snow, that stood out above everything else. Something in the appearance told me that it was not natural. I moved behind it, so I couldn't be picked off by some sniper from down the hill. I poked around with my entrenching tool in the side of the mound, and what a surprise! I hit a concrete wall. I then summoned some of my men to join in and scrape some of the snow off to see what we had. It turned out to be an old observation bunker, used by the Belgian army around World War I. This area was a former artillery range. We were careful to stay behind the bunker, while we continued digging and clearing the snow only on the back side. The more we dug, the more exciting it became. As we got near what was originally the top of the concrete bunker, I noticed that part of the top had been removed.

This was tailor-made for my platoon CP. We dug a little more and discovered that the opening was just large enough to crawl into the bunker; however, the bunker was still full of dirt. Everyone pitched in and shoveled, and shoveled, until we removed all the dirt from inside the bunker. We ended up with a nice eight by ten foot concrete pill box. Three quarters of the box still had an eight inch roof of concrete. As I searched further between the roof and the front wall, I found an opening about the size of a football, still filled with dirt. I was careful to pull the dirt in rather than to put it out over the clean snow. I was assuming that the hole went all the way through and was hoping that it did. Within minutes, I ran into

My platoon during our first break after the Battle of the Bulge. Men who are not in photo were doing their laundry in a nearby creek.

snow; then I knew that it went all the way. I also pulled the snow inwardly and soon we not only had room for CP, but also an observation post (OP) for our artillery forward observers, John Mehaffy from Texas, and Richard Byers from Ohio. This was really an FO's dream. He could direct fire down on the German line, and not be seen by them. The snow in front of the pillbox had not been disturbed except for the small observation hole, and I'm sure it couldn't be seen from the woods some five-hundred yards down the hill.

By now other divisions had gone on the attack from the center and the right side of the Bulge. By the end of January, the Bulge had been straightened out, while we, the 99th Infantry Division, held the northern shoulder on the Elsenborn Ridge. The front line now ran generally along the border almost as it had on December 16, 1944. At places, though, some other division, such as the 82nd Airborne, had penetrated through the dragon's teeth and large pillboxes that made up the Siegfried Line. By this time the Battle of the Bulge was considered finished.

CHAPTER 17
The Longest Night

D uring the early part of February 1945, the entire 99th Division was pulled off the line at Elsenborn Ridge, Belgium and ordered to advance toward Germany. It wasn't until we arrived at the Siegfried Line that we learned that we were to relieve the 82nd Airborne Division. Our 3rd Battalion, with Company I leading, reached the first Dragon's Teeth by dark. These were large concrete obstacles resembling dragon's teeth built along the entire German-Belgian Border by Germany to hinder any intruder from easy access to their country. Captain Morris came up to me and informed me that because of darkness, the entire battalion, except my platoon, was going to remain on this side of the Siegfried Line. I was to take my platoon and make the relief, and the remainder of our troops would join me at daylight the following morning.

I had no idea how large a unit I was to relieve, or where they were located, except the general area. It was so pitch black by now that it was difficult for each soldier to see each other just a few feet away. We moved forward slowly in a single file. I remember reading an article once about similar darkness during World War I, and the men, in order to remain in contact with each other, took their rifles off their shoulders, then, the forward man held the muzzle end of the rifle of the man in back of him with one hand, and the butt end of the rifle of the man in front of him with his other hand. I immediately ordered each man to do the same, and we managed to remain together as we moved forward throughout the Dragon's Teeth. I had heard so much about the Siegfried Line, and now here we were going through it. I felt almost like a tourist if it had not been for the war.

The Dragon's Teeth occupied a flat area of about two or three hundred yards in a valley on the border. Then the ground began rising up toward a hill or high ground and again a forest. I just felt this, from our walking, since our visibility was almost zero. A pathway had been broken through by tanks and explosives. With the exception of being dark, it was fairly easy walking.

Halfway up the road, which started from where the Dragon's Teeth ended, was a large pillbox, the size of a house. One large concrete room, possibly thirty by sixty feet, with a very high ceiling. A young paratrooper was standing guard at the entrance. He informed me that the battalion CP was located inside and the battalion CO had been waiting for me. The room was semi-dark; the only light was emitted by a lantern sitting on a table in the middle of the room. The CO was standing next to the table with a telephone and map. He appeared to be much over six feet tall. This was a battalion of the 508th Parachute Regiment. A unit with much pride and *Esprit de Corps*. I saluted and reported, identifying myself and my platoon. His first question was, "How many troops do you have?" I replied, "A platoon of thirty-four men, sir." As soon as I spoke, I thought that he would go through the roof. He was outraged, and I didn't know why. He continued by asking, "Do you know how many men we lost taking the ground up there yesterday?" pointing in the direction of the hill. I replied, "No sir." He said that they had lost some 250 to 300 killed in yesterday's action, and he was not about to let me complete the relief, with only one platoon of men. It just dawned on me. I was to replace what was left of his entire battalion. I informed him that the rest of my battalion was going to join me at daylight, but this didn't budge him.

During his rampage, I got the feeling that I was guilty of something, and had done something wrong, but I couldn't blame him for the way he felt. He then grabbed his field phone, and called his commanding general, General Gavin, and informed him of the situation. Because of suffering so many casualties, he didn't feel it was a good idea or safe to let me relieve his battalion. With only my platoon defending, the Germans could retake the hill with a major attack. General Gavin informed him that the division had another mission, which was already planned, and that the battalion's relief had to be completed by two o'clock a.m. the following morning.

The lieutenant colonel quieted down a bit by now, and was almost solemn. He appeared sad and disappointed that he had to allow the relief to be made. He quickly informed me that he was unhappy that he couldn't keep his men there until the next day. He then told me that the most he could do, under those conditions, was to leave a telephone with me which was connected back to corps artillery. This meant that the guns which could support me were at least of the 155 mm size. He said the phone would remain hooked up, at the front line position. He also showed me two concentration numbers on the map that I could call for, when and if I needed them. With that, he shook my hand and said, "May God be with you." I went out into the dark, picked up our guide, who was a young paratrooper, and we were on our way. After walking uphill for several hundred yards, the hill flattened out as we again could feel it by our walking. We looked towards the sky and could tell that there had been several shellings there, since most of the tree tops were missing. It also felt as if we were walking through a partially open field.

One of my newest young replacements who joined my platoon that day walked close to me so that he could get used to his new environment. He had trouble walking, and was stumbling quite a bit. He remarked that he thought he had just stumbled over something soft, like a leg or other body part. I knew what it was, after what the battalion CO had told me. To put my man at ease, I said, "It must be pine tree limbs, with their needles." The area had been shelled the day before, and many trees and limbs had been felled by artillery fire. I couldn't tell whether he was convinced or not, but he seemed to be relieved with my reply, as we moved on.

We soon arrived at what had been a company CP. There was a bunker with a telephone, which I was happy to see. A sergeant met me. His company officers had all been killed during the previous day's fighting. He informed me that all of his men were packed and ready to move out, but were waiting until we arrived. He was so relieved that we were there, since he could now gather what men he had left and depart. What devastation, what a battle it must have been. I could feel the pulse and heart of every paratrooper there.

I had my men wait around a while until most of the paratroopers moved out. I did not tell them that our platoon was going to replace an entire battalion front; I didn't want to burden them more than necessary. I thought that, in case of an attack, we had a better chance of survival if we were positioned in a smaller perimeter defense rather than in a long line of foxholes formerly occupied by the battalion.

I kept Sergeant Rosen, my platoon sergeant, and Private First Class Wetherby, my runner from New Hampshire, in my immediate area. Then, I had the remaining thirty-two men take positions around a small rise in the ground around my CP. My bunker was included in the perimeter defense. All the men began digging through the snow, and the thawed ground underneath, in order to obtain some protection in case of attack. My work and worry was now only beginning.

I commenced immediately to call for artillery from corps. I first called for both concentrations that the colonel had given me. The shells came overhead within seconds, and exploded several hundred yards ahead of our positions. I now felt that we had some sense of security. Every twenty minutes, during the entire night, I called for either one or both concentrations of artillery at once. Sometimes, I would ask for minor corrections, and could tell by the explosions that the artillery had responded to my requests. I changed my pattern so that the Germans could not mass an attack at any specific moment. I just wanted to keep them unsettled. I also changed my interval at which I called in. All night the Germans were extremely quiet, and my men were likewise. I sweated every moment out, contemplating an enemy attack. Just before daybreak during one of my shellings, we heard a great commotion of pots, pans, horses and wagons out of control over at the enemy lines. I was sure we must have hit their kitchens.

I thought that the night would never end. Thinking that if a German unit of battalion size or larger ever attacked, our goose was cooked. I kept up the interdictory fire until daylight, with no response by shelling or attack by the enemy. I knew they must have been licking their wounds. I was ready to continue the barrages, but as I looked to the rear, I saw a column of our troops with Captain Morris leading and the rest of the battalion following him. Our battalion had arrived, and not a minute too soon to suit me. Captain Morris asked me if everything had been quiet. I replied, "Nothing unusual happened, J.J." Little did he know that this had been truly "the longest night" of the war.

CHAPTER 18
Going to Paris

C aptain Morris had a smile on his face, seeing that all of us were safe. I couldn't have been happier than seeing all of my battalion arriving. I provided J.J. with all the information I had learned from the Airborne Battalion CO. He directed the assignment of all the company, and then sat down to a great meal of K-rations.

At about ten o'clock in the morning a call came in from the regiment requesting that an officer be sent back for R & R in Paris. Captain Morris looked at me, and asked if I wanted to go. He didn't have to ask twice. I said "yes" before he could change his mind, and I was off and running. What a surprise after such a tension-filled night.

I walked back through the shelled area that we had traversed the previous night, and was so moved at what I saw. It was truly a killing field. Throughout the entire Battle of the Bulge, I had never seen such a sight. There were several hundred paratroopers, all young, some all intact, some were in parts, lying in the field. All were heroes. All had given their last full measure of devotion, just the same as President Lincoln expressed in his Gettysburg Address. I thought I was already hardened by the war, but when I saw this, I couldn't help but feel a deep sense of sorrow, and great respect for all those fallen comrades. Their dying was the reason for my being alive, I thought. I had to stop and pause for a few moments, as an act of respect. I stood there silently, with my thoughts, not alone, gazing over the field. I was so moved, I know I shed a tear or two.

After a few moments I continued back down the hill to the large pillbox. It was now occupied by Lieutenant Colonel Moore, our battalion CO and his staff. The airborne battalion CO and his troops were long gone. A driver with his jeep was waiting for me. I jumped into the jeep, and the driver took me back to regimental headquarters. There, I loaded with some fifteen or so officers and men on a $2^1/_2$-ton truck, with a top on it, and off to Paris we went. A major was put in charge, so he rode in the cab up front with the driver. We made a stop at a billet at Rheims, France. It was late at night, so there was no time for sightseeing. After breakfast the next morning, we continued on to Paris, and arrived there about noontime. We were billeted at the Louvre Hotel which was not too far from the Paris Opera House. We had a hot meal first, and then we were on our own. First on my order was a hot shower. Completing this, I put on some clean clothes, and tidied up a bit. A subway station was located just around the corner, which made it handy if we wanted to travel around the city. I was surprised at the weather, being much warmer than in the forests of the Ardennes. It was quite comfortable to sit on a street bench or walk about the great avenues.

I decided to just sit on one of the benches along the walk near the subway station and watch the Parisians walk by. My first focus was on several men with poles six or seven feet long walking along the platform and occasionally reaching down into the subway well, along the track, and coming up with a cigarette butt stuck to the end of their poles. The poles had a sharp nail inserted into their ends, and looked similar to the ones used by our maintenance people in America to pick up papers and other debris in the parks. I knew we had cigarettes rationed in the U.S.A., but this was ridiculous. The men had a pouch tied to their belt which was used to deposit the butts as they gathered them. They walked back and forth along the platform, and almost fought for good areas when the trains arrived. I couldn't help but think of the cache of cigarettes I had back in my hotel room, and what barter I could be making.

The walk was full of "ladies of the night" in their short skirts walking to and fro. Some had an American GI or officer at their arm, walking to some area of their choosing. Some "ladies" were still empty handed but available and beckoning for business. The last one I saw was a lieutenant colonel of maybe sixty years of age and his friend of equal age. This surprised me, but age is not a detriment to happiness. They looked happy and smiling as they passed by. I finally got tired of watching the Paris scene and went back to my room for some needed rest. I was soon informed that about twenty of us officers had tickets for the evening performance at the Folies Bergiere. All of us jumped at the opportunity and went to see the show of shows that first night.

The theater was packed with Parisians as well as Allied personnel. The program was outstanding and an eye opener. I had never seen anything like it. All the skits were on the risqué side and provided many laughs, some that almost brought the house down. The most surprising thing to me was the beautiful statuelike show girls that stood motionless along the back of the stage and on boxes or platforms of various heights. They were almost totally nude, with their well-developed breasts completely exposed. I asked how this was permitted in a regular theater. I was told that it was allowed as long as the girls didn't make any movements. We were in Paris, where one didn't know what to expect next. All my life I heard so much about their women, love and music, so I guess this show wasn't that revealing. The show finished, we again loaded up on our $2^1/2$-ton truck and returned to the hotel. I hit the sack, after one drink at the bar, and conked out for the entire night. I guess I was still fatigued from the battlefield.

I woke up during the late morning, and after breakfast I just loitered around the hotel. After lunch, another lieutenant and I went by cab up to the Paris Opera House to check on its schedule. Upon walking up the steps towards the front, we were very disappointed, when we looked and noticed that the building was boarded up, and closed for the duration. The cab took us back to the hotel, and on the way we heard a loud crash when the cab was rounding the corner. The driver pulled over to the curb, stopped and got out. He then walked to the middle of the street and returned with a round piece of metal like a stove top. We also got out to see what had happened. On walking to the rear of our taxi we noticed smoke coming out of a large upright, round tank or stove next to the trunk. For the first time I learned that our taxi was fueled by coal. We had just lost the top to the stove, our power source. The driver replaced the top and off we went to our hotel. We couldn't travel too fast, but for wartime, at least, coal was still available and cheap. We arrived at our hotel, had dinner and spent the remainder of the night resting.

The next morning three of us obtained a guide, a middle-aged lady, who seemed to know everything, including the English language. She took us by cab to a central area, near an Egyptian obelisk, and then she had us walk, and walk, and walk everywhere we went. The Eiffel Tower, the Seine, and the most important place that I wanted to see, the Palace de Invalids and Napoleon's tomb. By one o'clock we were bushed and only too happy to get back to our hotel. We arrived at our hotel and looked around for something to do. Someone mentioned the Piggale, or "Pig Alley," as we Americans called it. It was supposed to be the most exciting place in Paris. That evening three of us got the subway and took off for the excitement Piggale had to offer. The first thing that struck me was how easy it was to ride the subway and knowing where you were at all times. This was because there was a map on the wall, made out of colored tiles, at every station. The map showed the station you were at, the one you just passed, and the one you were going to next. The tiles were so large, we couldn't help noticing them even though we didn't know French. Very shortly, we arrived at the Piggale Station and detrained. Upon walking up the street we got the impression it was Mardi Gras. The streets were just jammed with walkers. Many Allied personnel, peppered with natives, made up the crowds; however, most of them were GIs with their girlfriends.

We finally decided to enter one of the nightclubs, and found it so crowded we didn't think we could fit, but a young waitress immediately led us to a small table, no different than the ones you'd find in a New York night spot. We crowded around the table and ordered drinks. Music was already playing, but within minutes a woman singer came out and entertained us. She sang in French, which we didn't understand, but she made many gestures which we did understand, and we joined in the laughter with the rest. I had the feeling that all her songs had a story to tell, and she acted each one out along with her singing. We spent a couple of hours here, drinking and watching the show and then took off for our hotel. We had some satisfaction, knowing that we had now seen at least some of the Paris night life. We slept late the next morning, and then couldn't help thinking about our returning to the front and the shooting. By mid-afternoon we again found ourselves in the $2^1/_2$-ton truck, and on our way, rested up, and knowing that we had been in Paris. I had expected more. We arrived at Rheims, and were billeted for the night in an old building. While we had a little daylight left, all of us went and saw the great Rheims Cathedral. It was so impressive, not only for its size but also for its beauty. Every niche and corner of it had something different to offer. The only disappointment I have, is that at the time I had no idea that Rheims lies in the heart of the Epernay District of France. This is where their fine champagnes are made. Now, being an amateur wine maker, I would really appreciate it.

The next morning, we were off and running again. Our ride got colder, and colder, as we neared Belgium and more so the Ardennes. I joined my company, and was surprised to learn that our regiment was pulled back from the Siegfried Line, and occupied an area near Losheimgraben. The regiment was now assigned as the division reserve. Here everyone had a chance to clean up, get refitted and get a much needed rest.

CHAPTER 19
In My Footsteps

We remained in the area of Losheimgraben only several days and then moved to the Aubel area. This was the first staging area for the division when it first arrived in Belgium. Not only our 394th Regiment was there, but the entire 99th Division. We were now designated as the First Army Reserve. It was now mid-February and the weather was beginning to let up a little.

Within a week our much needed rest was over, and we were committed to the front once more. This time we were going to initiate the drive on the Rhine. The end of February was near.

Our first operation took place in a field leading into Germany on the eastern end of the Ardennes. There were about one hundred yards of open terrain next to a road. This led into scrubby type small trees, eventually becoming the normal large fir forest.

Our battalion was organized for the attack in line of companies, with Company I on the left, Company K in the middle and Company L on the right. There was still about a foot of snow on the ground, but the weather was beginning to warm up. The waiting was very tense. This was considered more of a mop-up operation prior to reaching the Cologne Plains. We didn't anticipate too much enemy action. We required no artillery pre-shelling support, so we knew that the enemy was not too strong. A good feeling prevailed. This feeling didn't last long though. Soon orders came for us to advance. Company L's first scout started out to advance on our right. As soon as he advanced a few steps through the snow, a "jumping Betty" mine exploded and wounded his foot and leg. His moaning carried in the cool afternoon air all the way towards our line. The hurt was felt by all. It seemed that the attack was halted and nothing else was happening.

Company K was next to move out. Their first man led the way and the same type of mine exploded. His leg was also blown off by another "Betty." Apparently we were in the middle of a mine field and no one knew it. You could feel the tension mounting when his moaning also reached us. Things were at a standstill for a moment. Then Captain Morris informed me that it was our turn to move out and my platoon was to lead.

We were already lined up properly with my scout right in front of me standing in the snow. The moaning from the two wounded men to our right could still be heard. I ordered my scout to start forward. His face turned pale, and he started trembling. I ordered him again to move out. Instantly, he collapsed into a sitting and crouching position in the snow. I knew he had reached his breaking point; however, this was not the time for delay. I had a feeling that if there was any further delay, the men, all shocked from the moaning and the uncertainty of what mines lay ahead, might bolt and not advance. We had no mine detectors.

I instantly summoned all the men around me, and told them that I was going to lead, and to "follow me," but further, to follow in my footsteps and not to step out of them under any circumstances, unless I stepped on a mine. My "moment of truth" had arrived. I knew as the platoon leader, I had to do it. There was no other way out. I could imagine that I too would step on a "jumping Betty," but I tried to picture myself a super officer and moved out. This was the moment to prove myself.

Snow field near Krinkelt, Belgium, similar to the snow-covered mine field through which I safely led our entire company.

Photo courtesy of the Department of Defense

The most difficult moment was when I lifted my left foot and slowly placed it down on the snow for the first step. The snow crunched as I gently shifted my weight over to that foot as I sunk deeper and deeper. Nothing happened when my foot reached as low as the compressed snow would permit. I was so relieved that I had not stepped on a mine. I repeated the action with my right foot and nothing happened. I turned my head around, and reminded my men not to get careless and step out of my footprints. I paused, and continued the procedure, left foot, then right foot, and so on.

As we neared the woods I got more confidence, but not once did I change my pattern, either by the size of my steps, or the intensity in which I was stepping down. Always slowly, always gently. I finally arrived at the edge of the scrub oaks, and thought that the mine field, if we had come through one, had ended. Logic told me that it would have been a very difficult task to lay mines between the small trees and bushes in the woods ahead. Nevertheless, I was still careful until I reached the tall tree area. I stopped, turned around and was happy to see that all my men and the rest of the company were coming through safely by way of my footprints.

Before long we were in a tall fir forest, advancing towards our objective, which was a couple of knolls several miles northeast of us in Germany. We were also relieved that we didn't encounter any enemy, not even a sniper on the way. When we reached our objective we dug in on the high ground and remained there for two days.

After two days, orders came to disengage ourselves, leave our position and march back to our earlier jumping-off point. We started back, following an old trail which ended up just to the right of the spot from where we had jumped off two days earlier. During our two day stay on our objective a slow drizzle fell on us, and before long, only spots of snow remained. Most of it had melted away.

Before long we were approaching the old area from where we had started several days before. The same gnarled pine and other points that I recognized were there. A shock came over me when I looked down on the ground to our left and paralleling the road that we were on. Right before my eyes, as far as I could see, was the field that we had traversed covered with a net of rope. The net had squares of about one meter or less apart. On each side of each square, a mine was attached, the shape not different than a stick of dynamite and maybe twelve inches long. These were the "jumping Betty" type mines. To think that I must have stepped in the center of each square, without setting any mines off was incredible. It was unbelievable that our entire company had traversed the entire field without any casualties. On seeing all of this, I felt a nervous electrical sensation all over me. I looked up to the heavens, and didn't know what else to do, but to thank God. It was truly a miracle. We must have had his guidance.

We moved down the road on to another assembly area, not too far away. On the next day our drive through the Cologne Plains started in earnest.

CHAPTER 20
Birth of Our Flag

As we began attacking across the Cologne Plains, we encountered very little enemy resistance. However, the going was very slow, because of the quagmire left by the early spring rains.

It was now early March and our casualties continued to be very light. Most of our casualties were the result of mines and booby traps left by the retreating German Army.

After almost three months in the combat zone, and trips to Verviers, Belgium and Paris, France, I had not seen an American flag. For the first time I had time to think about something other than fighting. I missed America, my home, my family and our flag. After all, our flag represented everything that was dear to me.

I called Captain Morris, my CO, and requested that a flag be issued to us for display in the field. He then called higher headquarters and forwarded my request. He was informed that we were not authorized to have one, and therefore denied my request.

The denial made me so furious that I thought to myself, "If they won't give us one, we'll make one." I would wait for the right opportunity, and then would start on our worthy project. When I mentioned my idea to the men, all got excited. All were as enthusiastic about it as I was.

119

We continued attacking eastward and soon arrived at the town of Elsdorf on the Cologne Plains. The small towns and villages were falling, one after another, as we reached them. Best of all, casualties continued to be light or nonexistent. We soon crossed the Erft Canal, and arrived at Mullenburg, the town with the biggest display of white surrender flags I had seen to date. White flags were hanging from all windows. The town was partially evacuated, and the only enemy action was an occasional shell of artillery landing somewhere in the town. It was late afternoon and the artillery shelling ceased. We were then informed that we were to spend the night in place. The Germans were now well ahead of us and moving fast toward the Rhine. Their main objective now was to cross the river and prevent being trapped on this side, and captured.

Since this was our first break, I thought, why not start our flag now? I went up to several windows on the first floor, along the street and pulled down three or four of the white flags. I took them back to a large house that I had picked out for my platoon, and stretched them out on a large double bed. I brought some of my men around me and told them what I wanted to do. All were happy with the idea and immediately volunteered for the different tasks.

After looking over the white sheets, I focused on the one that I thought would be the proper size. I had no idea what the measurements should be. I knew that if it looked in proportion to other flags I had seen, it would be okay. I picked one sheet which appeared to be between thirty inches or three feet by five or six feet. All looked at it and agreed.

In this large bedroom were two good-sized red pillows and one blue set of curtains that reached all the way to the ceiling. They came down first. Then one of the men cut one of the puffed up pillows open, and what a problem we had on our hands. The pillow was stuffed with eiderdown, and the minute it was cut open, the down began flying out all over the room. If we talked, it blew; if we laughed, it blew; if we breathed, it would enter our mouths. Soon the bedroom was one entire cloud of eiderdown. We soon had to open the window in order to breathe. The down became attracted to the window opening and moved into it and outside, also forming a cloud outside the window.

In order to tame the flying eiderdown, we tried placing wet towels all over the place and tried to collect the small unsettled particles, with some success. When the cleanup was completed, we yearned for a sewing machine. One of the men went down the street and soon was back with a small machine that we could use. Some of the men began cutting out stars from leftover white sheets. Some cut out the blue background from the curtains. Some cut out the red stripes from the pillows. Our project was well on the way.

I appointed Bill Junod from Michigan, who was the platoon guide, to be the caretaker of the flag during its making. Since he was the platoon guide, his position on any march was always the last man in the rear, or the last in any attack. I thought that this would be the safest place for our flag to be. Junod found a good canvas pouch large enough for the flag and some of the material that we had not yet used. With almost a quarter of it finished, he packed the flag into his pouch and everyone, except the guards, sacked down for the night. This was not done, though, before one of the men took the sewing machine back to where he had "borrowed" it.

The next morning after eating our K-rations, we resumed our movement to the East. We must have captured five or more towns without incident until a sound which we had not heard previously confronted us. We had just been subject to ack-ack fire at ground level. When we were closing in on an enemy anti-aircraft unit, its men became resourceful, lowered their guns and fired on our ground troops. We sustained very few casualties, since some tankers moved in from our enemy's flanks and disposed of the ack-acks. They captured the gun crews and our attack continued. This had the likeness of just a mopping-up operation.

That evening we camped in a field near one of the towns and spent the night without any enemy encounters. This type of operation continued for two or three days. Each night I would ask Junod how the flag was. He would always say, "okay sir," with a big proud grin on his face. The next day we captured several more towns, ending up with a few enemy snipers killed or captured. We found ourselves resting in small farm-type houses at the edge of one of the towns. All information received from our scouts and headquarters was that the Germans were still way ahead of us and moving fast toward the Rhine River. Here was another opportunity to continue working on our flag. This time our medic John Marcisin, and Sergeant Rosen went out looking for a sewing machine. They came back within about twenty minutes, but they also had a young *Fraulein* with them, who was the owner of the machine. Sergeant Rosen could speak some German, so when he explained to her what he wanted the machine for, she became so interested that she wanted to help do some of the sewing. I didn't have a good feeling about this, so I told Sergeant Rosen that she could stand by, and be an observer, but that she could not work on the flag. She seemed to understand and the men continued with our project. I was so happy that night. With candlelight, one side of our flag was completed.

When we got up the next morning, I didn't lose much time in telling Sergeant Junod to bring out the flag, even though half finished. We displayed it over a window sill with its white background against the wall. We soon had many GIs from other companies as well as our own company come by and swell with pride, looking at our platoon flag. I know morale was up just as soon as the troops got a glimpse of Old Glory.

We enjoyed our rest there only until early afternoon, when orders came to move out again. I checked with Sergeant Junod about packing the flag and safeguarding it, and he already had it in his pouch, slung over his shoulder. The enemy was moving very fast in front of us, and we encountered only spotty resistance. This resistance was caused by some rear guards whose duties were to delay us so that their main body could safely cross the Rhine. Everyone was thinking that the war would be over soon at this rate of activity. One of the towns I remember well was Berghein. We stopped overnight and again occupied one of the better homes in town. It was vacated. The owners probably joined the German army as it retreated.

Sol Greitzer, the company runner from New York, spent much time with my platoon, when the company was resting or when he had nothing to do at the company CP. That evening in Berghein he remarked that he wished he had a violin to play. I had no idea that this seventeen year old was a violin player. I had another man in the platoon, Private First Class Rutherford from Appalachia, who was a fiddle player. For a moment I was hesitant as to what to do, since I didn't want to show preference. Personally, I enjoyed all music from classic to country.

I sent Sergeant Rosen with Greitzer to make contact with the *Burgermeister* (mayor) of the town and borrow two violins, assuring the mayor that we would return them when we were through with them. They were lucky and within minutes they came back with the two instruments. I gave one to Greitzer and one to Rutherford.

I had Greitzer go into one large room at one end of the house, and Rutherford at the other end, in an equally large sized room. Then we passed the word around throughout the platoon that we were going to have a concert, one with classic music, and one with country music. The streets were being guarded by some other units, so we didn't have to worry about enemy patrols slipping through.

Both had a "full house" to start with. Greitzer on my request played "Danny Boy," but also some beautiful classics. Likewise, Rutherford played great hillbilly songs. It gave me a great sense of satisfaction to know that in time of war all of us could still enjoy a few moments of music. Even though the men initially went to the room that offered their first choice of music, after a while they changed rooms and listened to the other side. Pretty soon we had soldiers from outside our platoon join in the audience. Although both groups seemed to enjoy their music, it was very noticeable that the room with the country music was louder, and soon some of the men were even square-dancing.

Rutherford told me that he had no formal music training, that he picked up the fiddle on the farm and played for fun, for his friends and neighbors at hoe-downs in his home town. On the other hand, Greitzer had studied music at the Julliard School of Music in New York City. Other than that, I didn't know much more. After the war, I learned that Greitzer had his debut at Carnegie Hall at the age of thirteen years. He played with Conductor Leonard Bernstein and was a viola player of renown. And to think that his modesty prevented his telling any of us about his talent and background. How lucky I felt to have such men, each with his own capability, each fighting for our country, and in my platoon.

In this town we were very fortunate to stumble into a small square building the size of a one-car garage. When the door was opened, brand new German field shoes dropped out. The building, packed to the ceiling with that hobnailed footwear, had to have been an enemy supply store. During the Bulge, when we needed a pair of shoes or boots or other items of wear, we were always told that the rear echelon kept them all. This was just the opposite of what we were told at Normandy. There, they said everything was being sent to the front lines. Needless to say, when we started our drive to the Rhine some of us were in dire need of shoes.

With this shoe warehouse, we thought we found heaven. Anyone who needed shoes fitted himself up with a pair. I was amused when I looked inside of the ones that fit me, and saw size forty-five. I knew it had to be the European method of sizing shoes. The hobnails were a little hard to get used to, but I managed.

The next day or two still found us moving closer to the Rhine. We went through so many small hamlets, and the only firing we were hearing now was so distant. We finally arrived at the Rhine River near Dusseldorf and Cologne near the Neivenheim-Gahn area. We stopped back from the river some one half mile or so according to my map. In fact, we couldn't see the river, but after studying my map I knew that it was close and to the east of us.

I asked Captain Morris, if I could take a jeep and driver and go search for the Rhine. He approved my request and we went off immediately. I could see on my map that we were close, but I wanted the satisfaction of actually seeing it. I followed my map and directed the driver what turns to make. Then we came up against a large slope to the east and our road leading up to it. I had the driver take the road, and to my surprise, as soon as we reached the top, I felt like we were at the edge of the Grand Canyon, but on a smaller scale. There in front of us and far below was the Rhine River. More shocking than that was that in a large flat area across the river, and directly across from us, lay what appeared, for the moment at least, to be the entire German army. I'm sure it didn't take me a second or two to tell the driver to put the jeep in reverse and pull back off the bank. He did that, stopped, parked the jeep, and we both walked back up the back of the hill in a crouched position. On reaching the top we both lay flat against the bank, so we could take a better look, and yet not be seen by the enemy. I felt like an Indian Scout of our

Type of "Flak" gun that was lowered and used against us on the Plains of Cologne.

Old West, looking down on a campground of covered wagons, with settlers and army personnel combined.

There must have been several thousand troops, including trucks, trailers, artillery and other military-type vehicles. It appeared that they were in an assembly area and were just resting, and cleaning up themselves and their equipment. I got the impression that they had just arrived there not too long before our sighting. I really doubt that they ever saw the jeep when we first exposed ourselves. It seemed that they were too busy cleaning up to be preoccupied with anything else. We didn't stay too long. I wasn't too happy to have seen so many troops, but satisfied that at last I had seen the Rhine. I returned and immediately reported my find to Captain Morris.

My find apparently was not so important, since those troops were no threat to us. They were on the other side of a fast moving river, and there were no bridges in the area which they could use to cross. Our concern with this problem didn't last long, after my reporting. Word had just been received that some American unit had already crossed the Rhine at Remagen. We remained in this general area for a day or two, then were loaded on trucks and were off as fast as possible towards Remagen and the bridge.

CHAPTER 21
The Remagen Bridge

W e arrived at Remagen on the afternoon of 10 March 1945, and were stopped in the town short of the bridge. Headquarters directed that our regiment hole up in houses, farms and the like until they could squeeze us through the bridge.

My platoon bedded down in some hay in a barn not too far from the bridge. It looked great until we looked to the side of the barn and saw one of the biggest artillery pieces I had ever seen through the entire war. It was a 240 mm Howitzer, and was set up between the barn and another large building. No sooner had we rolled over on the hay for a little catnap then the gun would shoot one of its large projectiles across the river. It seemed that the gun fired every ten or fifteen minutes during the entire evening. Not one of us was able to sleep. By ten o'clock that night our orders came to move out. We marched out in single column and continued this way until we arrived at the bridge. There, all the men were ordered to pick up one plank each from a big pile which had been placed there, I presume by the engineers. The men dropped off the planks as they were needed across the bridge. The planks were placed across the railroad tracks to make it passable for vehicular traffic. Going across was hazardous, since it was dark and we couldn't see too well. There

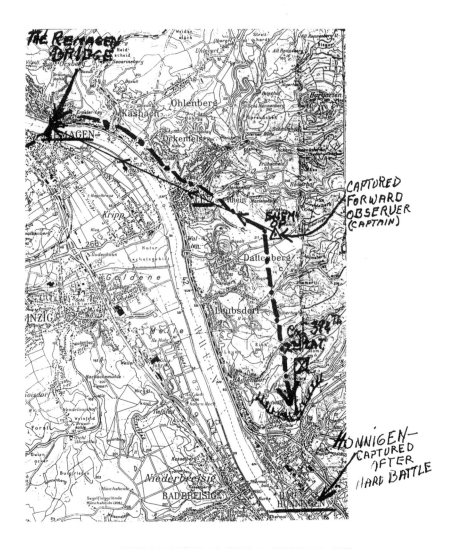

Map showing route of our fighting to expand the Remagen bridgehead south to
Honnigen. En route, we captured the *Wehrmacht* captain, forward observer, who
was directing artillery fire on the Remagen Bridge. This map was given to the
author by Jürgen Raths, former artillery officer, who commanded batteries that
fired on the Remagen Bridge during our crossing. We are now friends.

Map courtesy of Jürgen Raths, Bonn, Germany

Remagen Bridge as it appeared on 10 March 1945 when we crossed it.

Photo courtesy of the Department of Defense

were large holes, at many places all the way across, some between the railroad tracks, and some between the tracks and the steel girders that made up the framework for the bridge. It would have been so easy to lose a man or two through these holes without noticing it. The shelling from enemy artillery was so intense at times that we had to drop down and take cover. Shells seemed to be coming in every minute or so. The frequent stops slowed up the crossing so much that it seemed like eternity until we neared the other side.

Luckily we didn't lose a man during our crossing, but as we were nearing the other side of the bridge, men, vehicles, tanks, and other equipment all seemed to come together, almost to a standstill. As I got closer and closer, I saw someone who stood above the crowd directing traffic. He was standing on the hood of a jeep or a large box so he could easily be seen. By the time we got to him I recognized him as being Major Boyd McCune of our 2nd Battalion. He directed us to turn right, and so we did. I noticed that now traffic was moving along pretty rapidly, thanks to Major McCune's prodding.

It was very dark by now but we plodded along the east bank of the Rhine, very content that we had crossed the Ludendorf bridge without any casualties. We headed south towards Linz, a town the size of Remagen and some four or five miles from where we crossed. We arrived in Linz around one a.m., dog-tired, so we holed up for the night in some of the empty buildings. I saw Sergeant Junod for a moment and asked him if Old Glory was okay. He replied, "okay," and pointed to his pouch which he was carrying. I just thought, even though it was finished only on one side, our flag was probably the first American flag east of the Rhine during World War II.

CHAPTER 22
The Remagen Bridgehead

We stayed awake all night because of the shelling. So when daylight came we were ready to move out. Our company attacked up a hill which had very few trees and a few abandoned enemy foxholes. Some of the holes still had cover on them by way of bushes, limbs and grasses.

As I looked up the hill, about fifty yards ahead of me I saw Corporal Cannon from Pennsylvania walk up to one of the holes which was covered with bushes and grass. As he reached over to look into the hole a shot rang out and Cannon dropped over dead. He had been shot right through the temple. I directed his flank men to fire into the hole and not take any more chances. Upon clearing the debris we found a German soldier slumped over dead. The flank men had done their job. Cannon had done a very dangerous thing, without time to think about it. I ordered all the squad leaders and platoon sergeants to pass on to everyone in the platoon, "when in doubt—shoot first and explore later."

We kept moving forward with our attack until we arrived at the edge of a wooded area. We encountered some sniper fire but had no other casualties. The thought came to mind that we might hole up for the night, but Lieutenant Colonel Norman A. Moore, our battalion CO, got the idea for a night attack. This would be our first and our last night attack of the war. A night attack requires the utmost of control to prevent or minimize shooting your own men. I was surprised that one would be ordered now, through the woods. The orders soon came and the attack began slowly and methodically. We had to make sure everyone kept in sight of each other for good control. We managed to get through the woods without casualties. If the woods had been full of the enemy the story would have been different. After one hundred or so yards of walking, we came upon a clearing again and an incline that led to the ridge of the hill overlooking Honnigen. This was our objective on the next day. We dug in for the night. Throughout the night I remained on the alert for any possible enemy counterattack. We encountered no further enemy action.

Early the next morning we heard a lot of machine gun fire from up the hill but some distance to our right flank. The fire was being directed against some of the other units attacking the right side of the hill. Assuming that the Germans were probably dug in on the ridge for a last-ditch stance, I suggested that we precede our attack with an artillery bombardment. At first, my suggestion was not received too favorably, but after explaining that we might save many lives, it was approved. After all, all of us infantrymen were taught at Ft. Benning and other schools how the artillery could and should be used. This was a perfect condition, I thought.

A call was soon placed for the artillery, and in seconds it was flying and whistling over our heads. It was like the sound of music to me. As soon as it ceased we jumped into the attack. After much anticipation, we arrived near the top of the ridge without hearing a shot being fired. Upon our reaching the top, we discovered four large machine gun emplacements, with their guns destroyed, and four or five enemy soldiers in each emplacement, all dead from the shelling. The artillery had done a superior job, and just what we had hoped for. I couldn't help but think how many casualties we could have sustained, without the artillery, with those machine guns pointed down our throats.

We took our positions along the ridge line. One could see the town of Honnigen straight down to the south of the hill, and the Rhine to the southwest. There were machine gun emplacements several hundred yards down the hill, as well as some snipers. Our men soon found out that they couldn't even peek over the edge of the ridge. Any peeking invited either a burst of machine gun fire or a shot from a sniper. After several men were wounded everyone remained low and more cautious about their movements.

After the first day of capturing our objective, we had our first visit by a news reporter. I believe he represented our *Army Times*. Anyway, he was a very tall man and slightly built. A runner brought him to my position, and the reporter informed me of what he wanted to do. He wanted to look over the right edge of the cliff, and see Honnigen below. I told him that we already had several casualties there, and that it was too dangerous. He responded that he wanted to take a chance. The runner and I took him over to within twenty-five feet of the edge. We lay down against the ground and watched him walk slowly to the edge. Large bushes marked the entire edge of the ridge. No sooner had he started to peek over the edge of the bushes that a sniper's bullet hit the biceps of his left arm. He dropped to the ground in a crouched position. My sergeant, whose area the reporter was in, grabbed him in a hurry and brought him back to where I was waiting with the runner. All he could say was, "Am I lucky!" "Am I lucky!" I called our medic, who placed a large square bandage over the wound. The runner then took the wounded reporter back to the Aid Station. I'm sure he learned that even though we were occupying the highest hill north of Honnigen, it was still a dangerous place.

Machine gun fire was coming in over the edge of the ridge every few minutes. We now knew to stay down, and therefore incurred few casualties. This, though, was offset by incoming artillery fire, and our casualties in the company rose to twenty-two in just a two-day period. "Smoky," our medic, had the busiest two days in the entire war caring for our men.

Two soldiers from our Company I, 394th Infantry Regiment manning foxhole on hill overlooking Honnigen. (March 1945)

Courtesy of 394th Inf. Regt.

On the third day on this plateau we were ordered to shift over to our left by about one hundred yards. They were trying to straighten or adjust the line. We moved to our left and dug the needed additional holes. I formed my platoon inside the edge of a sparse forest of pines. We had just settled down when we heard heavy enemy artillery coming in. A sergeant and another soldier who was his assistant had just dropped in for a visit. They were to survey our location for a possible Observation Post for their artillery. Sergeant Rosen and I were talking to them when enemy artillery shells again started coming in. All of us hit the dirt in a split second. We received a tree burst, which is the worst kind, right on top of us. We had been standing in a circle maybe three or four feet apart. First was Sergeant Rosen, then the artillery sergeant, then me and finally the visiting sergeant's assistant. When we hit the ground we landed with our heads toward the center, and formed sort of a cartwheel. The first shell came and went with no damage. The second shell came, and after it hit the trees, its shrapnel came down among us with a vengeance. I heard a faint moan, and looked over to our two visitors, one on each side of me. They were completely decimated by the shelling. The sergeant was dead, but the assistant to my right had both arms completely cut off near the shoulders. I yelled for our medic. The man's eyes were in a daze and not focused. I lifted his back up as I crawled next to him, and held him next to me trying to comfort him. I told him that he was going to be okay, but I don't think he even heard me. His eyes rolled and closed, and by the time Sergeant Rosen came over with the medic, the man was dead.

I felt so helpless, holding this man whom I had seen for the first time, and not being able to help him. Death was so sudden, and yet with only several feet separating Sergeant Rosen and me from them, neither of us even got a scratch. After crossing the mine field, and now this, I thought sure my days were numbered. It was difficult to understand, but I do believe in destiny and this must have been ours.

The artillery had lifted, and I just visited our line to see if we had received any other casualties. Glad to see there were none in my platoon. I had Sergeant Rosen get some shuteye, after he had assigned every other man in each foxhole to be on guard while the other one slept. They would alternate every two hours.

I stayed up until approximately three o'clock a.m. During my waking hours, I made rounds and visited every foxhole to see how everyone was doing. Half of the men were awake and on the alert for any enemy patrols that might attempt to infiltrate up the hill and through our lines. The other half were fast asleep and getting their much needed rest. No coaxing was necessary.

Around three o'clock a.m. I awoke Sergeant Rosen and instructed him to continue in what I had been doing. I hit my bunker, and believe I was asleep before my head hit the ground. When dawn was breaking, Sergeant Rosen abruptly awakened me, and informed me that we had almost had it during the night. He thought that a German patrol had penetrated our lines during the night. He said that all of us could have been killed. I asked him how he knew, and to show me what he meant. He led me to one foxhole, then another, and showed me the footprints of someone with hobnailed shoes. They were imprinted in the soft mud, at the entrance to each hole or bunker.

I knew whose footprints they were immediately. They were mine, but I didn't let him know. I let him carry on, and after visiting three or four holes, I couldn't let him suffer any more. I nudged him on the shoulder and pointed down to the sole of one of my shoes, while I balanced myself and turned the sole up. He stopped for a second, embarrassed, but he started to laugh. He now recalled when many of us picked up German shoes on the Plains of Cologne. I'm sure he was quite relieved that the tracks were not those of a German, but of an American. I guessed that after several days of intensive pounding by the artillery I was due for a little fun.

After several days of frustration for not being able to silence the machine guns at the bottom of the hill, I called Captain Morris. I asked him if I couldn't go several hundred yards to our left on the ridge line and try to search and destroy the machine guns with our mortars. After some persuasion, he agreed and I began planning my operation. It meant that I would have to locate an observation post and remain there all day and be obscured from enemy sight and fire.

It was already morning and daylight. I obtained a field phone. Then I had the signal men bring up a large spool of telephone wire. They were to keep the spool in their position at the platoon area. I tied the end of the wire to my waist and began walking toward my objective, carrying the telephone. I had to remain behind the crest of the hill to keep the enemy from seeing what I was up to. The ridge sagged a little after I left our area and then leveled out again. After several hundred feet it went into a steep slope to the north. There were no enemy in the area, but there were numerous foxholes which probably had been vacated when we captured the hill.

When I reached the area near where I intended to establish my observation post (OP). I knew I could not move on top of the ridge or I would be exposed. So, I lay on the ground, with telephone in hand, and with the wire tied to my waist I began crawling and stopping, crawling and stopping. As I reached the top of the ridge, I stopped and looked ahead. Right in front of me I saw an empty foxhole, previously used by the enemy. It was about fifty feet down the forward slope of the hill. I flattened myself out, and felt like a piece of scotch tape attached to the ground.

I don't believe I have ever moved slower in my life. I began my crawl, knowing that I would be safer once I reached the foxhole. It seemed like an eternity until I reached my objective. I was also concerned about enemy soldiers coming up the hill from my left, trying

Looking down on Arenfels Castle and the Rhine River from my old platoon position of World War II. Honnigen, Germany is at the southern limits of the Remagen bridgehead.

Arenfels Castle (1993) still showing scars of war received from our 394th Infantry Regiment during the expansion of the Remagen bridgehead.

to reoccupy their old holes, or infiltrating our positions on top of the hill, from that side. I continued my snail pace and in time I was looking down into my foxhole. In order not to make any different movements than I had been, I continued crawling forward into the foxhole head-first. When I reached bottom I was so relieved that I had made it—hopefully, without being seen by the enemy. In addition, I still had the wire attached to me, and my telephone, carbine and field glasses were still in one piece. I settled down for a minute or two and got myself together. I then looked at the spectacular view below and could see the sloping hill to my right, slowly merging into the town of Honnigen below. I then began searching the hillside with my field glasses for enemy gun positions. It wasn't long until I caught sight of three or four enemy soldiers in a round revetment, which appeared to be a machine gun nest.

I hooked up my field phone and immediately called Captain Morris and informed him of my find. Also, that I wanted to place some mortar fire on the emplacement and destroy or dislodge the guns. We agreed to use the 81 mm mortars. I studied my map and gave my coordinates to the mortar section. The first shell was soon delivered. It was way off target, so I adjusted. The next one was closer but still not there. Once more I adjusted my reading, and over came the third shell. It landed and exploded very near the position. I then called "fire for effect." A large volley was immediately delivered. All the shells exploded in and around the gun position. One man seemed to be hit and didn't move, but two of them picked up the gun and walked at a fast getaway pace to their left. They continued walking until they went around the other side of the steep, sloped hill. There, they became masked by the hillside, and were out of my sight. I knew that from their new position, they would not be a threat to our company, since their new line of fire would have to be almost straight up.

Although I felt that I had accomplished my mission, I didn't want to reveal my position by moving. I informed J.J. that I thought I should remain there all day observing and go back to my platoon as soon as it got dark. I had just become an observer for a day.

As darkness fell, I disconnected the wire from my field phone, so they could start reeling it in. I picked up the phone, and my other equipment and started back to my platoon area. We didn't knock out all the machine guns (MGs), but at least I helped dislodge one of them.

In the meantime, while our battalion was doing its duty holding the hill overlooking Honnigen, the other two battalions of our regiment were attacking along the river on our right flank and at the base of the hill on the approach to the town.

On or about the 16th of March, Company K of our battalion, which was deployed to our right between us and the Rhine, began their assault on Honnigen. Their sector was the eastern third of Honnigen. Company K's colored platoon, which had already distinguished itself in its few days of battle, accounted for the major portion of prisoners taken and capturing that portion of Honnigen assigned to them. This was the first we had heard of colored troops

Remagen Bridge as it appeared on 17 March 1945 when it collapsed behind us while we were fighting to expand the bridgehead east of the Rhine River.

Photo courtesy of the Department of Defense

in our sector being assigned to front line combat duties, and they proved themselves with distinction.

On the 17th of March, information came throughout the lines that the Remagen Bridge had collapsed behind us—the result of all the artillery shells, aerial bombardments, and just heavy use. It just could not withstand any more. Now the feeling was that we had to fight much harder to hold on to our bridgehead, since we felt stranded, not knowing that the engineers had already built several pontoon bridges that were already in use. Once we were informed, the extra worry left us. After several more days, we were ordered to move out of our bridgehead and push towards the Rhur.

By the 18th of March our regiment had cleared and captured Honnigen. We then were pulled off line, came down the hill on the right side, between it and the Rhine, and wheeled around to our left. Once we reached the flatlands, we joined the other battalions pushing south and southeast of the town. The bridgehead had held, and now was being expanded. Our Company I followed with mopping up operations and we were soon breaking out of the Remagen bridgehead and on to the Rhur.

Some of my men displaying "our" flag for the first time on the east side of the Rhine River, near Remagen. (March 1945)

CHAPTER 23
Breakout to the Rhur

W
e kept pushing southeast until we reached the Weid River, at which time we were relieved by elements of the 2nd Infantry Division and we reverted to a reserve status, for a much-needed rest. During this rest period one of my men was scouting around the town that had been almost completely evacuated, and came upon the town's smoke house. I couldn't believe my eyes at what I was seeing. It was new to all of us. Right in the middle of the large one-room house was a wall, maybe three feet high, forming a round table of some ten feet in diameter. On the top of the table we could see literally a mountain of white eggs. It had to be the town's egg market. Against the wall was a chimney, with only three sides finished, black and full of suet. At the base was a fire pit but no fire. About five or six feet up, the three-sided chimney became a full four-walled chimney. One of the men looked up into its cavity, and made a beautiful discovery. He found a good sized ham hanging there. He immediately took it off its hook, brought it down and laid it down on a table next to the egg supply. Besides being a rest area for us, it also became a place to feast. I had Sergeant Rosen inform every man of our find and to join us. A fire was built in the fire pit. I made sure that no one wasted any of the eggs, but invited each one who wanted to cook himself a slice of ham and as many

eggs as he could eat. I couldn't believe it when one of the men cooked and ate twelve eggs by himself. After such a good feast all of us hit the sack in many empty buildings in the area and waited out the night.

The next day we followed the other regiments across the Weid River and attacked in a more easterly direction. That afternoon, our battalion was given orders to attack east and meet up with elements of the 7th Armored Division at the *Autobahn* which ran mainly from northwest to a southeasterly direction. Our Company I led the way, and my 2nd Platoon led the company. We traversed several valleys and hills during that afternoon. When we arrived on top of one of the last hills, fog and darkness set in on us. We stopped while I double checked my map. I noticed a little commotion between Captain Morris and one of the other company commanders of our battalion, after I had made a decision on what direction to travel. We were standing on a crow's-foot of trails leading in many directions. I walked about one hundred feet in each direction down each of the three or four trails and informed Captain Morris on which one of the trails we should take. Even in the fog, I had a good feeling for the topography and was very confident as to where we were. All that good training in map reading was now paying off.

It seems that the other company commander and two of his lieutenants with him did not agree with my decision. I again reiterated to Captain Morris that I was right on track and where we should be going. I was not going to follow the other officers in their direction. Captain Morris backed me up, and we moved out on the trail I had chosen. Night fell on us and we continued our march along the side of a hill. By four o'clock a.m. we arrived at our objective. It was now drizzling, so everyone just sat down in place and tried to keep warm. I informed Captain Morris that we had arrived exactly at our objective, so every man took a position and waited.

The 7th Armored Division was supposed to cross our front from right to left at about 5:20 a.m. As the time got closer and closer, it was also getting lighter and lighter. We soon could see the outline of the *Autobahn*. Captain Morris now knew that we were truly at the right place. This belief was further intensified when five o'clock rolled around and we could hear a faint noise of motors to the east down at the *Autobahn*. I walked down to the road and checked with the first driver and was informed that this was part of the 7th Armored Division. We were cut off and our job was done. All the men rejoiced by raising their rifles up in the air and yelling greetings to our fellow soldiers of armor. I never did learn where the other company that we left behind ended up, but I was satisfied to know that we were at the right place at the right time.

It was already the 22nd of March. We remained in reserve until around the 26th of March. During this lull, all the men worked mainly on their clothing and equipment. I checked with Sergeant Junod to see how our flag was doing. He remarked that he never let the flag out of his sight, and that it was always attached to his side in the pouch. I had him take it out, and we draped it over a limb, with the white side down. The location was right next to my tent in a lightly wooded area next to the Main Supply Route (MSR). The route was now being used to supply the 393rd and 395th Regiments which were advancing ahead of us.

General Lauer, our division commander, drove by on one of his inspection trips to the front and saw our flag. When he reached our battalion headquarters, he asked Lieutenant Colonel Moore, our battalion CO, jokingly who the little general was up the road with the flag. After Colonel Moore explained, he confided that "It was great to see the Old Stars and Stripes again." This was his first knowledge about our flag in the making.

On or about the 26th of March our resting days ended and our regiment was committed to the front again. We replaced one of our regiments which then became the reserve element of our division. Our mission was to follow the 7th Armored Division, and perform mopping-up operations. We went through many towns without firing a shot. One good-sized village that I remember was Wertzlar, the home of the Leica Camera and Optical Company. As we walked by the factory, we could see that the entire area was being guarded by MPs and other guard personnel from the 7th Armored Division. No chance to pick up any samples. Another town I remember well was Geisen. Here there was a pretty good size runway next to the road, and C-47 transports were already landing, with their resupply of gasoline for the armored column.

I don't believe we ever walked faster, trying to keep up, at least at a normal distance with the armored units. The enemy, whatever was left, was being demoralized, as evidenced by the increasing number of prisoners that were now being taken as the attack moved forward. We were also beginning to see more displaced persons (DPs) along the road walking toward us. These DPs, who were of many nationalities, had been captured from many nations and interned by

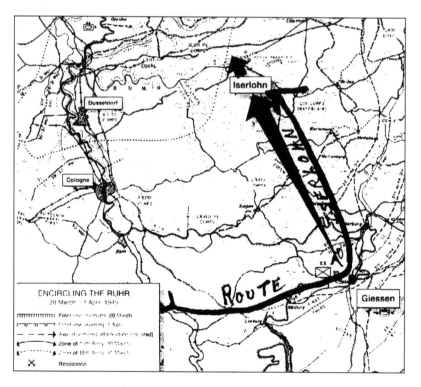

Map showing our route of fighting to the end of the Rhur pocket at Iserlohn.

Photo courtesy of the Department of Defense

the German army. All had been used as slave labor to satisfy the enemy's needs during the war. Soon the DPs were becoming such a problem for the American troops moving forward that they had to be collected and placed in camps. They were fed, housed and clothed and administered similar to a small community. The problems were much more complex because of their different ethnic origins. I didn't want any part of it. This duty fell on some other unit.

We operated throughout this area and covered many miles with few casualties. We were now beginning on our final drive north to close the Rhur pocket. We marched relentlessly from around the 4th of April throughout the 15th, through mountain ranges of fir forest. Every hill top was an objective. When we reached one objective, orders came to continue to the next one. German deserters were coming out of the forests almost everywhere we went and surrendering. I guess they knew their war was lost now and had then had enough. Our final object was Iserlohn in the middle of the Rhur.

We arrived on a late afternoon in the town of Hermner on the outskirts of Iserlohn. The entire attack stopped on the edge of a hill overlooking the town. No enemy activity was being observed, but Colonel Moore, our battalion CO, wanted to know what was ahead of us. I told Captain Morris that I would volunteer to go and explore the town to see if enemy troops were still there.

I took Sergeant Rosen with me because of his fluency in German. We walked clear around to our left flank and through the entire battalion area and then turned right toward the town. I was watching my map very carefully so that we would not get lost. We reached a main street which ran parallel to our battalion front and must have been two to three miles away. This was truly a "no man's land."

The streets were completely deserted, not a sign of life was seen. After walking about four blocks we came up to a two-story building, with a German ambulance parked behind the building. I told Sergeant Rosen that I could hear people talking inside. I started up the stairs with Sergeant Rosen covering me from the rear. I now had second thoughts on whether we had bitten off more than we could

Colonel Jeter, CO 394th Regiment pinning Silver and Bronze Medals on me during our ceremony east of the Rhine River. (March 1945)

chew. Were we walking into a trap? As soon as I reached the top of the stairs I could hear Germans talking. As I cleared the top with my carbine at the ready, I came face to face with two German medical Officers, and two nurses.

One officer, who spoke English, explained that they were medical personnel and unarmed. They were in the midst of packing their medical supplies in large boxes for their departure. After our assurance that no weapons were on hand, I told them to hurry up, pack and leave. Not knowing what was still ahead of us, I didn't want to be burdened with an enemy aid station on my hands.

Sergeant Rosen and I backed off, and still on guard, walked down the stairs and out into the street once again. The streets and homes still appeared deserted. We continued on our way with guns still at the ready, worried about possible snipers who may have been left behind. After several blocks, a horse and wagon appeared in front of us down the road. We stood behind a building and waited until he reached a point just across from us. We both jumped out and discovered an old man driving his horse and wagon. He told us that he was going to his farm up the road somewhere. We both boarded the wagon and ordered him to turn around. He gave us some argument about having to go to his farm. Sergeant Rosen spoke louder and with more authority and the farmer apparently got the message. He turned around rapidly and off we were again, this time riding to our destination instead of walking. I was still concerned with possible enemy snipers. Both Rosen and I lay down flat on the

Colonel Jeter and his 394th regimental staff at an award ceremony east of the Rhine River. (March 1945)

bed of the wagon right behind the driver and, looking at my map that I had flattened out on the floor, directed the farmer where to go.

We came to a big intersection and told the driver to turn right. I was sure this would take us back to our lines, but was not sure what lay between us and our units. It was getting darker by the minute, so Rosen told the driver to hurry his horse up a bit. We soon were in a slow gallop toward our front. We slowed down to a walk as we neared our front lines. A challenge was soon heard from one of our soldiers. I not only replied with the proper code words, but I also identified ourselves by name and unit. I wanted to make sure there were no doubts in the challenger's mind as to who we were. I can imagine their concern about a galloping draft horse and wagon coming directly at them. I'm sure this was a possible first in wartime.

Once recognized, we got off the wagon. Sergeant Rosen told the farmer that he should turn around and go to his farm. The farmer complied rather quickly. We walked across our line of infantrymen, and right behind them on the road lay a lineup of our tanks. A major stood on top of the first tank and apparently had been there all afternoon waiting to attack. He hailed me as I walked up closer to him. He questioned me as to how many enemy we had seen, if any, and their positions. When I informed him about seeing only the aid station, which by now had probably moved out, he raised his arm, turned to the remainder of his tanks and yelled, "Move out."

Sergeant Rosen and I stepped to the side of the road, and watched the tanks go by at a pretty good clip. I thought knowing that no enemy were out in front must have been some relief to the major. It also must have contributed to his tanks moving out so fast.

It was dark by the time we reached our company command post. I reported our findings to Captain Morris, and he in turn called Lieutenant Colonel Moore. We remained in that position the rest of the night. After the fact, I felt that I should have made my initial report to Captain Morris, instead of the major with the tanks. I have always thought that risking our lives with our patrol in no-man's land went unnoticed. I'm pretty positive that the major received credit for his spearhead, and capturing the empty town of Hermner.

The next morning we got up early and moved out to our final objective of Iserlohn. Within the hour we were there on the side of a hill, next to a German hospital. After sitting on the bank for four or five hours, we were told to move out to our right and load on trucks for our trip south. We had just witnessed the end of the Rhur Pocket.

CHAPTER 24
To the Danube

I t was already the 16th of April and German resistance was cracking on all fronts. The Rhur Pocket had yielded its share of prisoners while we suffered very few casualties of our own.

We rode for two days toward the south, then stopped and camped for several days near the city of Bamberg. After cleaning up and resting we found ourselves on trucks once again and off towards Nuremberg. Just south of the city, we were dropped off. This was the last ride we would get until after the end of the war. From this time on, which was near the end of April, we walked and walked and walked, day and night. During the first two days of this march toward Landshut we covered some sixty miles. We could always hear the German army ahead of us going the other way in wagons, trucks and other noisy vehicles. They were always able to remain some distance away and therefore we were never able to engage them in combat. During the crystal clear night their sound seemed like they were just several hundred yards away. I finally told Captain Morris, "I bet that the Germans think we never sleep." J.J. replied, "In fact, we never do." This came at the end of our sixty miles, two-day march. After thinking about it, no matter how tired we were, it was better to keep the enemy moving and off-balance than to stop and shoot at each other.

We were held up a little at Dietfurt and at the Ludwig Canal. The battalion suffered only a few wounded. We knew that the German army was fighting a weakened rear-guard action, by keeping a few men back, firing a few rounds of ammunition, and taking off again.

Looking at my map before reaching Landshut, which was our objective, we would have to cross the Danube River. We were encountering very little or no resistance and couldn't walk fast enough to reach the great Blue Danube. This was the river that all of us had known from the music we had heard all our lives. As we approached the high ground, I knew from the map that it couldn't be much farther. We reached the summit, and what a disappointment all of us experienced. At last the Blue Danube lay in front of us, but it wasn't blue, it was a muddy brown.

The small town of Heinheim stretched in front between us and the river. It was built right on the river's edge. We had another 1,000 yards or so before we could reach the town. During our final 500 yards or so, we encountered several old men in uniform who surrendered. They had no weapons and were part of a home guard organization. Then a couple of young boys, also in uniform, came out of a house toward us and told us that they wanted to surrender. As one of the young boys walked up to me, I placed my hand over his head like a father would and said, "Why, he's just a child." He was fourteen years old. I couldn't help but have compassion for such young boys being placed in "harm's way." When asked what they did for the *Wehrmacht* they replied that they were used as messengers.

As we arrived in town, we searched and learned that the town was void of any enemy forces, but we were still receiving artillery fire from the other side of the river. Captain Morris assigned our company to various buildings along the river bank, and told us that we would remain there for the night.

CHAPTER 25
Completing Old Glory

After all the men were satisfied that they really had seen "The Blue Danube" they returned to their quarters and ate their K-rations. As we were about to settle down, I thought what a great opportunity this was to complete our flag. The pontoon bridge under construction across the Danube would not be completed until morning. We were assured that we would stay here overnight, and were reasonably safe.

I sent Sergeant Rosen and "Smoky" in search of a sewing machine as usual. I don't believe fifteen minutes went by when both came dragging up the street carrying our much needed sewing machine. Smoky also informed me that we were short of red cloth for our stripes. During the search for the machine, he located some of the cloth, so he liberated it and also had it with him.

Seven of us were staying in the cellar of one of the houses closest to the bridge under construction. The cellar wall, on the side of the river, extended about six feet above the ground. There were two or three small windows equally spaced along this wall, from which we could see the river and its banks. We took several GI blankets and hung them over the windows. This was to prevent some artillery observer from south of the river from seeing our lighted cellar.

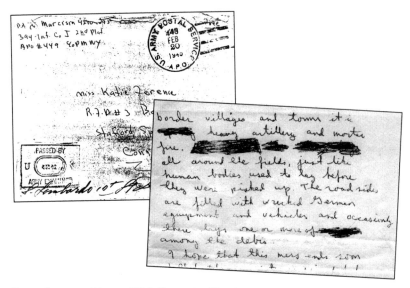

Copy of censored letter (V-Mail) sent by "Smoky" Marcisin to his fiancee during February 1945. I had to censor all letters sent out by our men at night in my fox-hole by use of candlelight, or gasoline burning in a C-ration can.

Photo courtesy of Mr. and Mrs. John Marcisin, Ashford, Conn.

The sewing machine was set up in a corner of the cellar farthest from the river. Sergeant Junod came forward with his pouch containing our unfinished flag, and little bits of material. Sergeant Rosen also joined us, and with him he had two large candles which he had also liberated during his search for the sewing machine. He lit the candles and set them up on some tall wooden boxes near the machine. What a picture this made, with all of us around our unfinished flag, working to get it completed by candlelight.

Our group consisted of myself, Sergeant Rosen, Sergeant Junod, Private First Class Wetherby, Private First Class Belair, Private First Class Beauvois and "Smoky" Marcisin. Belair operated the sewing machine and the rest of us cut out and handed him the needed materials. What a thrill it was to know that on this night, we would finally complete our "Old Glory."

Occasionally we could hear an artillery shell exploding. Several shells hit between us and the river, but in the cellar we felt pretty secure. Several more shells were heard exploding in the town but were too far away for us to be concerned.

After several hours of cutting and sewing, cutting and sewing, our flag was completed. It was such a beautiful sight, even by candlelight. It was getting late now. We admired our treasure for a few moments, then Sergeant Junod folded it carefully and properly inserted it in his flag pouch.

All of us, dog-tired, curled up in various parts of the cellar and tried to get some shuteye. We didn't hear any more explosions from the enemy artillery, but we did hear noises coming from the river all during the night. The noises were the results of the bridge construction by the engineers.

CHAPTER 26
Crossing the Danube

The next morning we were "up and at them" before dawn. My platoon was introduced to a new mode of travel. We were to ride tanks for our push across the Danube and on south. Four men were assigned to each tank and rode piggyback. I rode in the lead tank next to the driver.

Our drive south was spearheaded by the 393rd and 395th Regiments. Our regiment, the 394th, reverted back to a reserve status. Our principal duties now were to mop up the stragglers and POWs along the way. Being a true infantryman, I didn't like to ride tanks. My feeling was again reinforced when I slid down inside and took a seat next to the driver.

I have never suffered from claustrophobia, but if I did, this would certainly bring it on, but it didn't. I felt so constrained in my visibility and movement. I knew that on the ground, I could drop down into a hole or lie flat in some depression and be fairly safe from enemy fire and free to move in any direction. Inside the tank, I had the feeling of being a sitting duck, if the enemy were shooting. After a half day of rough riding, my platoon was through riding tanks. It was now somebody else's turn. Was I relieved! The tankers felt so strong in tanks, but for me, give me good old terra firma, and the infantry.

Sergeants Lietz and Tallerico, from our Company I, during a break, showing off their rabbit fur jackets that were procured from an abandoned factory in Landshut, Bavaria, during our last drive of the war. (April 1945)

We were somewhere this side of Landshut, when we got off our tanks and began walking. As badly as I felt about the tanks, I'm sure the men were happy with their much deserved ride. We soon learned that we had another river to cross, the Isar. This presented no problem, since the 395th was ahead of us. They built a treadway bridge during their attack on the city and its capture. They also captured many POWs in their operation. As we entered the city, news came down that our regiment had liberated a German POW camp and released quite a few American prisoners. It was Moosberg.

As we moved through the other end of Landshut, we went by a multi-storied factory building. Several of the men entered the building to search it out and found no one in it. What they did find were piles and piles of rabbit fur jackets. The factory had been producing these jackets for the *Wehrmacht*. It didn't take long for the word to get around. When I was several hundred yards past the factory, I looked back, and it looked like some scene out of a medieval period movie where fur coats were the "uniform of the day." Almost every soldier had liberated a jacket for himself. Instead of wearing them with the fur turned in, they wore them inside out. All I could see were two columns of black, brown, gray and white speckled human forms coming towards me. It was some sight. This was the

Author, *right*, with Sergeants Sammy Oliverio, Al Dimperio, and Claude Rivers during a break from battle. Dimperio was our mess sergeant and had just brought us a hot meal. (April 1945)

time for the soldiers to relax. I don't believe this could have happened in any other army or at any other time. These were freedom-loving citizen soldiers, American GIs. This was around the first of May, and we were heading in a southerly direction again. By the next day we arrived near the vicinity of Muhldorf, crossed the Isar River and received orders to stop in place. We camped near the town of Peterskirchen in Southern Bavaria.

CHAPTER 27
End of the War

While at Peterskirchen, we were told that our next objective was Berchtesgaden, Hitler's hideaway. The scenery around our area was spectacular. The snow-capped Alps were in the background to the south. A patchwork of beautiful farms and villages were in the valley in front of us. There were no signs of the enemy. Everything was so peaceful. We knew that something was up, maybe the end of the war was near.

We remained in position for several days. Our preoccupation was getting comfortable and cleaning our equipment ourselves. "Smoky" heard that the area was full of a small type deer. It wasn't long until most everyone saw several small deer running across the field next to where we were camped. Since, as a medic, he had not been permitted to carry firearms during his entire duty in the war, he asked now if he could go hunting. I gave him permission to go hunting with the M-1 rifle, on one condition, that he shoot only enough deer for food and that he replace his "Red Crossed" helmet with one that was unmarked. He checked with our Mess Sergeant Sifford, and off he went. I don't believe he was out but a few minutes, when he returned with one small buck, the size of a kid goat. The mess sergeant had it prepared and all of us enjoyed a taste of venison. This was repeated the next day and "Smoky" was all smiles,

"Smoky" Marcisin, our medic, kneeling with two buddies, after a successful hunt in Bavaria, Germany at the end of World War II. He really looked forward to this day, since I had forbidden him to carry a rifle as long as he wore a helmet with the Red Cross insignia, and was carrying out his duties as medic. (May 1945)

contented that he had bagged two deer in two days. This was the end of our hunting season. The next day, May 8, the war ended for us. The war officially ended at 0001 9 may, 1945. We remained in this area, relaxing for several days. On one of these days one of our officers returned from a trip to Munich. While in the Munich area, he had the opportunity to visit Dachau, one of the former Nazi death camps. He told us what a terrible experience this had been for him. Seeing the ovens used in the Holocaust and the piles of dead Jewish people still in the area was almost too much for him. He took some photos of the area which he later developed. It gave all of us the understanding of what a terrible tragedy had occurred throughout Nazi Germany. To think that all of this had been kept a secret from us throughout the entire war. Their security must have been without flaws.

My men and I displaying "our" completed flag for an army reporter at Kitzengen, Germany. (May 1945)

Within several days we found ourselves on the move again. This time by trucks, our destination being the Main-Franken area for occupational duties.

CHAPTER 28
Occupational Duties

My platoon was housed in a *Gasthaus* in Markbreit, Germany, a town between Ochsenfurt and Wurzburg. We were just one-quarter of a mile from the Main River. Our principal duty was to run a jeep patrol once a day through ten or fifteen small villages. Consequently, we had a lot of time on our hands. The *Gasthaus* was like an inn with bedrooms, a bar and lounge. Once a day I would go to Ochsenfurt to a brewery and pick up our daily supply of beer. We were going to operate just like back in the States. In order to maintain good discipline and order, beer and wine would be available only after duty hours. The first day there, I had Sergeant Rosen assemble all the men in the platoon, and march them down to the town square. Here I had Sergeant Junod bring out our flag. I called everyone to attention and the Stars and Stripes was raised rapidly and proudly. That first day of occupation was a day to remember. In the afternoon we had retreat formation. Even though we didn't have a bugle or other form of music, we went through the ceremony. The men stood at attention and the colors were brought down. Sergeant Junod, with the help of one other soldier, folded the flag properly and put it away. We followed these procedures during our entire four week stay here.

I assigned one man to remain at the *Gasthaus* to keep an eye on things. He was also responsible for keeping the lounge and bar cleaned. While he was here, I would take the rest of the platoon down to the river and engage in athletics—volleyball, baseball or swimming. This was like a real Rest and Recuperation (R & R).

During the second day of occupation, the man I left behind to guard things came up to me running, upon our return from the river. I thought something bad had occurred. He called me to the side while the rest of the platoon went to their quarters. He guided me to a stack of cases of empty soda bottles which were piled against the outside wall of our building. He then went over to one side and turned on an electric switch. He asked me if I saw anything. "Yes," I said. I could see a line of light, the shape of a door. This is what he had discovered during the day while we were gone. We removed the empty cases, found a door, which I opened, and steps leading underground. My man had explored this already, but he wanted me to see our great treasure. After some steps, we landed on the floor of a massive underground wine cellar. Another set of stairs led us to another cellar at a lower level. What a find! The only

First Sergeant Cumstay, with other members of Company I, including Mess Sergeant Siewert, Privates Gudzan, Sol Greitzer, and Bellair, enjoying after-hours at our *Gasthaus* at Markbreit, Germany. (May–June 1945)

Captain J. J. Morris, myself, and two men from Company I, enjoying "our" flag while on occupation duties. (Kitzengen, Germany, June 1945)

problem I had now was to operate the bar on a set schedule, from after "duty," 5:30 or 6:00 p.m. until 9:00 p.m. The other problem was to keep the cellar under our control, so that other units of our regiment wouldn't visit, and help themselves at all hours of the day or night. We placed a lock on the cellar door and I placed my "Charge of Quarters" man in control.

We then announced, through channels, to the regiments that the wine was available after 2:00 p.m. every afternoon. That all units would be limited to five gallons at a time. By the next day a large convoy of jeeps and other trucks were lined up for their take. The system worked, and everyone seemed to be satisfied. Our flag raising and lowering ceremonies still were continued daily, although, every day the number of local spectators increased. By the end of the first week I believe half of the townspeople came down and lined up around the square to see "Our Flag." We had a feeling of having a little bit of America on the Main River.

Some four weeks were spent here, conducting patrols, engaging in athletic activities, controlling and dispensing the wine, and mainly goofing off. All of us were waiting to accumulate points in order to return to the States. One needed eighty-five points to be eligible. Most of the men had between eighty and eighty-five points. I had eighty-two. Points were given for the total service, service overseas, combat service, etc.

CHAPTER 29
Jail of Pleasure

While stationed at Markbreit, our company was responsible for several special type activities. Among these was the operation of the Ochsenfurt Jail. The jail was now being used for the internment of some two-hundred German women POWs. After several days of operation Captain Morris sent me to Ochsenfurt to inspect our jail. Lieutenant Thompson, platoon leader of our 1st Platoon, was in charge of the operation. As soon as I arrived, Lieutenant Thompson had me read one of the POWs Identity cards. It read "For the Pleasure of the Wehrmacht." As soon as Sergeant Rosen translated this we made a pretty good assumption that our POWs were camp followers. They followed the German troops in the field and provided the *Wehrmacht* companionship, and maybe something else.

Lieutenant Thompson had several NCOs assist him in his supervision of the jail. As soon as I arrived, he displayed disgust with his new assignment, and said the "ladies" were unruly and were going to present him with many problems. He was praying that either he or they would be transferred out of our area soon. As soon as he expounded his displeasure with his assignment we began walking down through the building, on our inspection.

The "ladies" occupied two tiers of bunks on each side of the corridor. Most of them were lying down on their bunks, and clad in only minimal clothing, sometimes with only a bra and panties. The few who were fully clothed were standing next to their bunk. Most of them were in a jovial mood, laughing and smiling and mumbling words, which went over my head. The entire atmosphere was certainly not one that you would expect in a prison. I understood why Lieutenant Thompson was unhappy with his assignment. It took the last ounce of self-discipline to keep our composure, one of being serious and not show any embarrassment. Everything appeared to be clean and in good order, until we reached the end of the hallway.

Standing there at the end were two sergeants from another unit, not ours. "How did they get past your guards?" I asked. Lieutenant Thompson was dumfounded, and had no answer. I then asked the intruders how they got there. One of the sergeants replied that he didn't enter from the front door through the lieutenant's guards, but secretly through a back door. Upon examining the situation we found that the door led to a tunnel, which led underground to the courthouse across the street. The sergeants, together with their company, were billeted in the courthouse. Once they found the secret passageway, they began a part time business, with our inmates and their fellow soldiers. Now, I understood why the women were smiling and laughing when we were walking through in the morning. They knew that they had been operating under our noses, and we had no knowledge of it.

I immediately ordered a lock placed on our side of the door, and our jail was now secured. Lieutenant Thompson was so relieved. I was also satisfied, but I don't know about the sergeants and the "ladies of the *Wehrmacht*."

CHAPTER 30
On to Nuremberg

At the end of the four-week period, orders began coming in for some of the men in our company. On seeing this, Sergeant Rosen informed me that the platoon was in formation outside the *Gasthaus*, and I was to see them. I guess we all knew that this could be the last time my platoon would still be intact. With personnel being reassigned daily throughout Germany, one had no idea how much longer we would be together. Sergeant Rosen called the platoon to attention. He presented the platoon to me and saluted. I returned the salute. Then he informed me that the platoon had something for me. Sergeant Junod stepped out from the end of the platoon formation, came up to me and presented me with our platoon flag. I was moved so much that I was at a loss for too many words. I do remember saying that I would take good care of it. The formation broke up, and everyone went about their duties.

Within a day or so my orders came as expected. I had no idea as to where I would be reassigned. When looking at my orders, I was really happy when I read Nuremberg. Upon my arrival I reported in to Lieutenant Colonel John T. Corley, a West Pointer, from the 1st Division. He had fought with the division all the way from Africa and was one of our highest decorated officers in the army. We were at the Palace of Justice, where the War Crimes Trials were going to be held. Lieutenant Colonel Corley was in charge of the overall operation. I was assigned to duties of building officer. The duties had no limitations as to what I was to do. Principally, I was to get the building ready for the trials, which involved supervising building repairs. There were several holes in the roof, results from our bombings. Repairing desks and other furniture and organizing the different rooms as they were needed. Colonel Corley had the first office as you entered the building. I had the second office, adjacent to his.

The first thing I did was to get a stand with a pole, and stood my flag up right behind the desk. Although I enjoyed having the flag and admiring it, sometimes its presence attracted uninvited guests. As they entered the building and came past Colonel Corley's office they saw Old Glory, and thought this was the principal office. I then would direct them to Colonel Corley's, and I would continue at what I was doing.

One of my first visitors was a middle aged German lady. She was beautiful, blonde, fair skinned, and looked well kept. She was carrying an orange, and an apple. I had no idea where she got them. We certainly weren't getting any with our rations. She approached my desk, and requested that she wanted to give fruit to her hus-

band, Colonel General Jodl, who was supposed to be in prison there. She was the wife of Colonel General Alfred Jodl, head of all German forces at the end of the war. We were not allowed to pass on any information about the future use of this building. Being caught off guard, I recoiled a little, and then informed

Adolf Hitler and Hermann Goering meeting during their heydays. Saw Goering almost daily while on duty at the Palace of Justice. He was now gauntly looking and escorted by two MPs.

Courtesy of the Department of Defense

her that I was getting the building ready for military occupancy, but had no knowledge about the trials.

She replied by saying that the *Stars and Stripes* in Berlin had published that the trials were going to be held here. I again said that this was news to me, and that I would not accept the fruit she was carrying. I didn't know whether or not she believed me, but she was satisfied with my answer and yet appeared disappointed as she was escorted out of the building.

The first rooms we had to prepare with urgency were five interrogation rooms on a second-story wing. These rooms were to be used by the prosecutors to prepare their cases. The prisoners, who were being detained in the prison located back of the Palace, would be brought in through a tunnel under the street, similar to the one

at Ochsenfurt, and up the inside stairs to the interrogation rooms. This was done every morning around nine o'clock. The prison was operated by the provost marshal, and I had nothing to do with its administration. I was so busy with my operations that I never had time to even visit the prison.

One day as I was on the second floor, walking by the interrogation rooms by the top of the stairs, a lieutenant colonel was directing traffic, and ordered everyone to stop and clear the stairs and

Field Marshal Wilhelm Keitel, chief of the German High Command of the Armed Forces (OKW), with Hitler. I saw Keitel almost daily while he was being escorted by two MPs from the prison to the interrogation room which I had prepared in the Palace of Justice at Nuremberg.

Courtesy of the Department of Defense

hallway leading to the rooms. I had a good vantage point, as I was standing right at the top of the stairs by the last step. I soon understood what the commotion was all about. Coming up the stairs was Hermann Goering, with one MP on each side of him. He was dressed in a tidy gray uniform, void of any medals or rank. His face was gaunt and his eyes somewhat hollow. He would take one step and stop, another step and stop. It must have taken him ten minutes to reach the top of the stairs. I was informed later that he was so weakened when they took him off drugs, and that's why he was walking so slowly. Within minutes, General Keitel came up, also accompanied by two MPs, except he walked at a normal pace. When he arrived at the interrogation room he saluted, clicked his heels and entered. One couldn't help but feel that he was still all soldier.

Von Ribbentrop, a former ambassador, followed Keitel in the same manner. The only difference being, when he arrived at the rooms, he shook hands with several people who were waiting for

Generaloberst Alfred Jodl, chief of the *Wehrmacht* Operations Staff, and one of Hitler's closest friends. His wife approached me and requested that I pass an apple and orange to him while he was in prison behind the Palace of Justice. Request was denied.

Courtesy of the Department of Defense

him. He was a reminder of a glad handed politician. This was the last time I saw any of the prisoners, since my duties picked up momentum, with the arrival of the other delegations. These were the British, French and Soviets. Among all of them, the Americans' secretaries from Washington were the most demanding. I got the impression that they had no idea that a war had just been fought, and that we didn't have all the supplies that they previously had in the States. In due time, I believe everyone was satisfied, and operations continued as usual.

I believe the most satisfied, on his day of arrival, was Chief Justice

Jackson, chief of the Tribunal. During my search of the palace soon after my arrival, I discovered some eight or nine grandfather clocks stored in the basement. I hired a clocksmith and had them all in working condition within a short time. I then had them placed in the office of each head of a delegation. I picked the best one and had it placed in the chief justice's office. It was ticking away when he entered his office for the first time. He walked straight over to the clock to admire it. You could see the twinkle in his eye and a sense of satisfaction. He then walked over to his desk and again he smiled when he saw a white telephone. I learned from his aide, the two things he admired most were grandfather clocks and white telephones. I don't know where his aide had picked up the white phone, but there it was.

I continued my work here for several months and had the building almost ready for the trials when I again received orders to move. This time to Hammelburg, Germany.

CHAPTER 31
At Hammelburg

The Hammelburg facility had been a POW camp for American prisoners and later for displaced persons. Now we were using it as an internment camp for German political prisoners. The first thing I did was to place Old Glory in my office behind my desk. There were six-hundred male prisoners, and all had been top dogs in the Hitler regime. They operated their own kitchen and laundry facilities. We kept most of them busy at cutting wood by hand using cross-cut saws. They were given 1,800 calories a day, mostly potatoes, and they were pretty much satisfied. One day the assigned camp commander, who had been a former mayor somewhere, complained to me that they were not getting enough salt for

My entire platoon in formation displaying "our" flag. Kitzengen, Germany (May 1945)

Prisoner of War Camp, at Hammelburg, Germany. Soon after our American POWs were released, it was occupied by 400-500 Germans (all political prisoners). I was then put in charge and served for approximately sixty days.

Photo courtesy of the Department of Defense

their food. Further, that he had a friend in a nearby town who had plenty of seasoning, that if I could send a jeep with one of his men, he could obtain the needed salt. After some consideration, I assigned a jeep with a driver and a guard, and they were off and running. About four hours later all returned happily with their loot. The bag of about one-hundred pounds in weight was on the back of the jeep. The salt was in rock form and not granulated, but it didn't matter to the commander. When he saw the salt, his eyes beamed, and with a big smile he came over to me and thanked me, bowing at the same time. A little bit of humanitarianism went a long way.

The camp ran without trouble the whole time I was there. The day before I departed for Marseilles, one of the prisoners came up to me and presented me with four pictures, about 4 x 6 inches in size, that he had painted in watercolor while in the prison. I accepted them and placed the pictures in a secure place. They were really of professional quality. He told me that he had been an artist. I departed the next day wondering whatever would happen to the six-hundred political prisoners. Some possibly were interned at other prisons, and some possibly freed.

Watercolor paintings made by a German POW at Camp Hammelburg, Germany. He gave them to me on my departure, citing my humane treatment of POWs.

CHAPTER 32
My Return Home

O n arriving in Marseilles, they didn't lose much time in load-
ing us on a ship for our trip home. It was now the 2nd of
December 1945. All we were hoping for was to get home
for Christmas. We boarded a Liberty Ship, named the *Tabita Brown*.
It was supposed to be the first Liberty-type ship built in Portland,
Oregon. During our trip, it didn't take
much to convince me that it was a first
ship built. We hit one of the worst storms
several hundred miles before reaching
New York. The ship had to go five-hundred miles south and out of the storm's
path. The worst part of the trip was,
when we were informed that Liberty
ships had a tendency of breaking in half
under such bad conditions as this one.
We were instructed where to stand in case
of such an eventuality. Our hearts were
in our throats during the twenty-four
hour ordeal, wondering when the
breakup would occur. By the end of the
second day of the storm, the seas subsided

Major General Walter E.
Lauer, Commanding General,
99th Infantry Division, under
whom I served during World
War II.

Courtesy of the
Department of Defense

Generals Eisenhower, *center*, Bradley, *left*, and Patton confer in the Ardennes.

Courtesy of the Department of Defense

somewhat, and everyone prepared for our arrival. It was now the seventeenth day since we had departed from Marseilles. The storm had delayed us three or four days. Nevertheless, we were so happy to be coming home, and I couldn't wait to see the Statue of Liberty, once again. Five or six of us officers were clear up front at the bow of the ship, impatiently waiting to get the first glimpse of the Lady. There was a light blanket of fog over the bay as we closed up to the harbor. Soon, some of the fog lifted in spots. Through one of these openings I could see, with pride and joy, our Statue of Liberty. This is what we had fought for. This was a moment to relish.

Fellow officers who made the return trip together on the Liberty ship *Tabita Brown* (first Liberty ship, built in Portland, Oregon). We punched each other on the upper arms when one would use profanity. It worked. By the time we arrived in New York, we had cleaned up our language. (December 1945)

It was our home, our America, with "Old Glory" flying "O'er the Land of the Free."

THE END

EPILOGUE

I was really dismayed when the Supreme Court ruled that burning or desecrating our flag was all right because it is an expression of free speech. I still don't agree with their decision. Expression of free speech involves only the individual, but when one desecrates the flag in any way, he or she is trampling or destroying something that belongs to all of us, and therefore I believe it is wrong.

It gives me great satisfaction that my men and I made "our" flag, and it is safely protected at our National Infantry Museum, Fort Benning, Georgia. At least this is one flag that no one will burn or desecrate.

"Our" flag on display at the Infantry Museum, Fort Benning, Georgia.
Photo courtesy of Dan and Sandi Scott, Fallbrook, Calif.